Let's All Laugh At

su

We hope you enjoy this one-off eigh[...]
full of jokes, articles, photos and pis[...]
the demise of our local 'rivals'.

According to the dictionary, rival(s) –
'with whom one competes' or 'to equal – to be as good as'

Are sunderland a rival of Newcastle United Football Club?
Is sunderland a rival of Newcastle Upon Tyne?
Is Elvis riding Shergar in next year's Grand National?

We'll meet again, don't know where, don't care when.

Thanks To
Mick Edmondson, Mark Turnbull, True Faith, Mark Templeton, Bob Murray, Stephen Walker, Hag The Mag,
Toon Army News, Mark Jensen, Mick Martin, Howard Wilkinson, Cheeky Monkey, Jimmy 'old jokes' Tarbuck,
Steve The Joiner, Steve Robson, Brent Pitcher, Paul, Keith Patterson, The Mag, Andy Edmondson, Brian
Johnson, Kev Milburn, Johna, Peter Reid, The Homes Of Football, Gary Kempster, Eminem, Alan Harrison,
Biffa @ NUFC.com, Vicky Cowan, Mike Smith and Comical Ali. Apologies to anyone who we failed to mention.

Design > Tommy Anderson

Further copies of LALAS (Let's All Laugh At Sunderland) are available at all decent newsagents
in the North East or by sending a cheque/P.O. for £2.99 a copy including postage, payable to -
LALAS C/O The Mag, Office 55, Design Works, William Street, Felling, Gateshead NE10 0JP

"*I've just flown in to sunderland airport*"

And some news just in...

A Mackem who threw his brother into the Crocodile pool at Lambton Lion Park has been prosecuted by the RSPCA.

Electricity reductions due to a lack of public funding on Wearside were so severe in sunderland today, that in the first race at sunderland dog track the Hare came third!

In court today a Newcastle fan complained in his defence that his work colleague who just happened to be a Mackem, had continually used threatening and abusive language towards him whilst he was driving along the A19.

Shouts of "You're going too fast you'll kill me you Geordie Wanker" and "You Twat, you're doing above 120mph" and "I'm shitting myself," were all words the Mackem is said to have used. Geordie continued, "To make matters worse my Lord, the swearing continued when I was untying him from my roof rack!!"

And some sports news just in, the Mackem who won last month's 'Tour de France,' has just completed his lap of honour and is now recovering in a French hospital.

There was an embarrassing incident at Madame Tussaud's

last week when sunderland boss Howard Wilkinson revealed a wax model of himself and his assistant Steve Cotterill drove it back to the Stadium of light by accident. Luckily it only held four team talks and attended two home matches before it was discovered.

Figures released today show that two out of every ten men on Wearside, work for a nationalised industry. While the other eight sit and watch them.

On hearing the above news, sunderland shipwright Albert Titmarsh aged 65 declared that he'd never had a day

Newcastle invasion of Roker Park

illness in his life - he always made sure he was off a week.

A survey on the decline of morals in Britain reveals that in sunderland alone on each day last week, an average of 292 married women made love to an unmarried man. The Geordie bloke is now recovering back home in Byker, Newcastle.

It was twenty years ago today that sunderland's one-eyed goalkeeper, Ian Hesford, the worst keeper the UK's ever seen, was involved in a road accident. Hesford who had let in over 150 goals that season, was heard to shout "I'm Shite I couldn't catch a cold," before he threw himself in front of a Double Decker bus......... luckily the Bus passed under him and he wasn't hurt.

Today at a factory in sunderland which mass produces Cheesy Chips, the prototype of a huge sixty foot high food mixer went completely out of control. The entire company has gone into liquidation.

Mick McCarthy has just announced the signing of a top Chinese international for sunderland at a price of £250,000; WY ME

It has been revealed in a sunderland hospital that a man was admitted today who had lost his whole left side. Doctors say he's all right now!!

SUNDERLAND AFC

Invite you to a

RELEGATION DINNER DANCE

(In aid of the ex-managers redundancy fund)

Starring

'GLENDA MILLER' & the 'SOUTHWICK MAJESTIC JAZZ BAND'

On 27th of May 2003
At Crimdon Dean Caravan park

* RAFFLES * BINGO * SPOT PRIZES *

1st Prize – a place in the team next season
2nd Prize – Tommy Sorensen's glass eye
3rd Prize – a 1st team four year contract

SARS VIRUS HITS ENGLISH TOWN!

The lethal S.A.R.S. virus which has claimed hundreds of people's lives worldwide, has struck in the North East of England, in the town of sunderland. The virus, which first claimed lives in Asia and Canada, has hit 'The Stadium Of Light' and as a result their football team will play in the first division next season.

SARS stands for 'sunderland Are Really Shite' as well as 'sunderland Are Relegation Specialists', so the Wearside area is riddled with the deadly virus. Large cities such as Newcastle, Liverpool and Manchester are safe from the virus as none of their football teams will play against sunderland for a long time. However, places like Wigan, Crewe, Gillingham and Rotherham will be in immediate contact with the Mackems and are already ordering surgical face masks. Also worried are places like Hartlepool, Colchester and Wycombe as they could be playing at the Stadium of Light in the 2004/05 season.

Experts predict that the virus could be also active in Sheffield and Shrewsbury where 2nd division bound 'Sheff. wed. Are Really Shit' and conference bound 'Shrewsbury Are Relegation Specialists'. However, neither of them have both symptoms so experts are hopeful that Mackemland is the only place it could strike so long as people stay away and if anyone shows any symptoms they are immediately quarantined. Thankfully sunderland is the least visited place in Europe and that shows by the fact they only have one hotel! A cheap Travel Tavern.

As a result of the epidemic sunderland will not be allowed to play in any Cup competitions and were to be banned from playing in Europe but UEFA have decided not to bother discussing the matter as there's no chance of them ever qualifying anyway, unless they won the fair play award.

JOKES

Q: What's the difference between a Mackem and a bucket of shite?
A: The bucket...

Howard Wilkinson is in Joplings department store in sunderland when he sees an old lady struggling with her shopping bags trying to open the door. "Here pet can you manage" he asks in his softly spoken voice. The lady turns, looks at him and snarls, "Here mate Fuck Off, you're the daft bugger that took the job."

Wearside Council planning chiefs today announced that they have found a major design fault with the Stadium of light. The main stand faces the pitch!

News has just broken that a Coach full of sunderland fans travelling to Walsall has crashed on the M6 motorway and everybody on board was killed instantly. Newcastle fans were gutted at hearing the news, as there were 7 empty seats.

Alan Shearer and Kevin Phillips were away with England in Holland when a prostitute propositioned them in a street in Amsterdam. Kevin asked her "How much for a little wank?" Then Shearer asked "and how much for a superstar?"

Snow White panicked when she heard that the local mineshaft had collapsed, as the Seven dwarfs were working there. She raced to the scene and when she reached the entrance at the top of the mineshaft, she put her ear to the ground and heard a small voice singing from down below.

"sunderland for the cup, sunderland for the title." "Thank God" cried Snow White, "At least Dopey's still alive.

Q: What's the difference between a dead dog in the middle of the road and a dead Mackem in the middle of the road?
A: There are skid marks in front of the dead dog.

Q: What's the difference between sunderland and Foot and Mouth disease?
A: Foot and Mouth got into Europe...

Q: What's the difference between Bob Murray and a battery?
A: A battery has a positive side...

A new Red and White Oxo cube is about to hit the supermarket shelves it's called a laughing stock.

Q: What do you call a Mackem lass who has an abortion?
A: A crime stopper

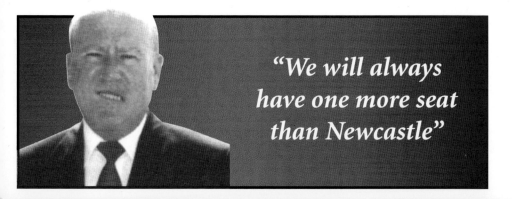

"We will always have one more seat than Newcastle"

sunderland 0
Arsenal 13

Report by Dick Dastard

An average Arsenal side narrowly beat North East Top Dogs sunderland this afternoon at a packed Stadium of Light. The atmosphere was electric as the two sides warmed up in the white-hot cauldron of noise. The crowd of 15,163 were ecstatic as sunderland won the toss and decided to kick-off against the champions who were without Ljungberg, Bergkamp, Campbell, Lauren and Cole. However injury hit, sunderland were missing only Marcus Stewart and boss Mick McCarthy who had a full squad to choose from, admitted he has had no luck with his crippling injury list, so unlucky are the Wearsiders.

The Londoners were lucky to take the lead against the run of play in the third minute when Wiltord scored with his head from their 9th Corner. Two minutes later Francis Jeffers beat 8 sunderland defenders and slipped the ball under the advancing Sorensen to make it 2-0 with the referee nowhere to be seen. Jeffers looked miles offside, as he picked up the ball outside his own box from Seaman's throw. However, the mackems were

having no luck and things got worse for them when the referee sent off 2 Arsenal players in the 9th minute!!

Arsenal's 9 players now had the advantage, as you know how hard it is to play against 10 men never mind 9!! And it paid off as they scored 6 more before half time with 6 lucky break-aways all against the run of play. Even at 8-0 down at half-time sunderland could count themselves unlucky not to be on level terms as they'd had 7% of the game.

The second-half got off to a flyer as Arsenal scored a ninth as a 57-pass move was luckily finished off with an Henry diving header. Then in the 61st minute sunderland put their best move of the game together, when Gray walked under a ladder, before finding McCann with a perfect 5-yard side footed pass. The midfielder, under no pressure, cleverly passed it back to Sorensen in the sunderland goal, who then hoofed it beautifully up the field and out of play. It just goes to show how unlucky sunderland are in front of goal this season as it would

have put them right back in the game had it gone in.

Then sunderland had more misfortune when Thierry Henry was stretchered off scoring Arsenal's Tenth. Unlucky sunderland were up against it as Arsenal were down to eight men as they had used their three subs. But with only 10 minutes remaining Phillips actually touched the ball and he found Kilbane who miss-kicked it to Tore Andre Flo who was in plenty of space, but he accidentally tripped over his bootlaces just 10 yards outside the box, yet the referee didn't give what was a blatant penalty. The Mackems were having no luck whatsoever for the 34th match in concession.

Arsenal went on to add 3 more goals before the end but sunderland can count themselves so unlucky, and will look back at that late penalty claim as it could have changed the whole match, and probably their season.

Whoever called them 'The Black Cats'? As they are SO UNLUCKY!

LET'S ALL LAUGH AT SUNDERLAND

JOKES

What do you do if a Mackem throws a hand grenade at you? Pull the pin out and throw it back.

What do you say to a Mackem in a suit?
"Would the defendant please rise."

Why should sunderland fans be buried 100 feet deep? Because they keep telling us, that deep down they're really good people.

Bobby Robson was walking down Dean Street when three Charva lasses approached him. The first girl flung her left breast out and shouted "here Bobby sign this." Bobby, being the gentleman he is signed it.
The second lass got her right breast out asking Bobby to sign it. Bobby signed it being the gentleman that he is. The third girl pulled up her skirt and dropped her knickers, bent over and shouted "Here Bobby sign this" To which Bobby replied "Get lost pet, only sunderland managers sign Bums.

Peter Reid walked into the changing room at the Stadium of light and noticed a big lump of shit in the middle of the floor. "Whose crap on the floor?" he shouts angrily. Niall Quinn stands up and says, "Me Gaffer, but I'm not too bad in the air."

A Mackem is walking along Whitburn beach with his scruffy, flea bitten one eared three-legged dog when he finds a magic lamp. So he picked it up, rubbed it, and to his amazement a magic Genie appeared in a cloud of smoke, "You have released me from 1000 years of torture being stuck in this lamp, for which I will grant you one wish," explains the Genie. The Mackem thinks about it for a minute before coming to a decision.
"I love my dog so I wish for it to become perfectly clean and healthy and to have four legs and two ears again.
The Genie replies, "I am a Genie but not a miracle worker!". So the Mackem comes up with another wish. "I'd like sunderland to qualify for Europe." The Genie looks at the Mackem and says, "Give me another look at that dog again.

What's the difference between a Mackem and a trampoline? You take your boots off to jump on a trampoline.

Why do seagulls fly upside down in sunderland? Because there's nothing worth shitting on.

What's the difference between a Washing Machine and a lass from sunderland? You can dump your load in a washing machine and it won't follow you around for a week.

"sunderland will be challenging for the premiership title in the 2003-04 season"

THE STADIUM OF LIGHT

The Fans they all flocked, to the very first game,
To the fancy new ground, with the shit fucking name,
They came in their thousands, the numbers weren't low,
The majority had come, just to see Status Quo,
The team they all knew this, so they just tried their best,
As champions from Holland, put the side to the test.
Bob Murray he just sat there, his head down in shame,
Cos he just admitted he thought of the name.

The Geordies they all scoffed, and the world it did laugh,
At the sunderland chairman's, huge fucking gaffe.
The rest of the board, they warned of the flak,
The mackems would take from the rest of the pack.
The laughter it was loud, the laughter it was long,
How can we make it fit into a song.
It may take a while, it may take some time,
To think of the words, with which it will rhyme,
No match with red, but a match with white,
But what springs to mind, it matches with shite,

At the end of the day Mr Murray was right,
To call his new stadium "The one full of shite."
Everyone out there was dying to score,
But the evening ended, in a predictable draw.
And so we close, with just one more laugh,
At the stadium in Blunderland, with a name that is NAFF.

TWO BOB'S WANT YOUR TWO BOB!

The 'Bank of England club' sunderland are a club in crisis as a result of Relegation into the first division. As a result of bad investment, bad management, and very poor performances on the pitch, the club who once bragged about being England's richest are in the same league as Wigan, Crewe, Gillingham, Walsall, and Rotherham. In fact they will be a club of the past if they don't hurry up and turn things around. With crippling debts of £40 million and very few paying customers, experts predict they will fold unless drastic measures are taken. A spokesman for Doctor Do little financial services says, "They are doomed."

So Bob Murray has signed up Sir Bob Geldof, the Brain behind Live Aid, to help raise some much needed cash for the 'North East's top Dogs' - the 'Black Cats'. The scheme will be called 'Two Bobs want your Two Bobs,' and he reckons if every season ticket holder gives two bob each then an initial £84.60 could be raised.

Then if we start charging Kids and Students a Fiver each we might lose 20,000 fans but we'd hope to make a £175 profit per match instead by 35 pupils sticking by us. As well as redundancies and other cost cutting exercises the main reason for bringing in Sir Bob Geldof is for his expertise and experience in fundraising and the great news is that the man behind Live Aid is bringing the idea to Wearside.

On July 17th 2003 'The Stadium Of Light Music Festival' featuring top pop stars from around the world will perform live on the pitch.

The Wurzels, Peters & Lee, Darts, Andrew Ridgley, The Barron Knights, One Hand One Heart, Jarrow Elvis, Showaddywaddy, Shakin' Shields, 'Belinda from Carlisle', 'Bobby Knoxall' and 'The Brotherhood of Man.'

Tickets priced £15 are available from all usual outlets.

Also over the close season the club hope to hold a 'SUMMER FETE' at the stadium to raise funds. Numerous stalls and sideshows including, Guess the new nickname, Tombola, Beat the keepers (Poom, Hesford and Perez), Bingo, Charity bed push with Reyna and a Blue Pop Stall.

"We have occupied sunderland cathedral"

Trampwatc

SUNDERLAND
ASSOCIATION FOOTBALL CLUB

SUNDERLAND AFC V ▮
24TH FEBRUARY 2002
SUNDERLAND STA

YOU WILL BE ALLOCATED £17 TICKETS BUT
AUTOMATICALLY ALLOCATED £23 TICKETS
MAY ALSO BE ALLOCATED SINGLE SEATS BU
ARE AS CLOSE TOGETHER AS POSSIBLE.

NUMBER OF ADULT TICKETS _____

NUMBER OF U16 TICKETS _____

(Maximum of three tickets only)
I enclose voucher 59 from my season ticket book,
and
I enclose a cheque payable to Sunderland AFC wi▮
Or
Please charge my Credit or Debit Card (not Amex

EXPIRY DATE

Signature ....

NOW PLEASE RETURN TO NU21, PO
NO LATER THAN 19th JANUARY 2002 – R
STAMPED SELF ADDRESSED ENVELO
YOUR TICKETS WILL BE DESPA▮
IF YOU HAVE NOT RECEIVED YOUR TICKETS BY
BEEN UNSUCCESSFUL AND

4th January 2002

**Extra Tickets Exclusively for Season Ticket Holders to see
Sunderland v Newcastle!**

Thanks to your fantastic support this season, Sunderland continue to be one of the best supported clubs
in the country, with an average attendance of more than 47,000 fans at the Stadium of Light. Indeed if it
were not for visiting teams not taking up their full allocation, we would be 99% full for this season. We
now have the highest number of female fans in the Premiership and the youngest average age of fan in
the country - a healthy statistic and one we're very proud of - making the Stadium of Light THE place to
be on a match day. Your support is very much appreciated, and to celebrate the New Year we are giving
you two EXCLUSIVE offers for the big games coming up.

The **Newcastle United derby match** is one of the biggest games in the world, and with your season
ticket, you have guaranteed one of the best seats in the house for this massive match.

As a reward for all of our loyal season ticket holders, we are offering you the chance to buy up to THREE
extra tickets at normal matchday prices for the game. You could be the most popular person in your
household or among your friends by applying for these tickets for the clash on Sunday 24th February,
and giving someone you know the chance to be there. We are trusting season ticket holders with the
safe distribution of these tickets, to ensure full segregation is maintained.

Tickets are **ONLY** available to season ticket holders and there will be no public sale of these tickets.
Applications will be processed on a first come first served basis. All you have to do is send voucher
number 59 along with a cheque or credit card details. Prices are either £23 for adults and £17 for U16s,
or £17 for adults and £8 U16s. Applications must be received prior to January 19th 2002 and we will try
to accommodate you in the area of your choice.

Please send your completed application form, together with your payment, voucher 59 and a stamped-
addressed envelope to **NU21, PO Box 165, Sunderland, SR5 1WF,** or hand them in to the
Sunderland AFC Ticket Office.

SUNDERLAND ASSOCIATION FOOTBAL▮
Registered Office: Sunderland Stadium of Light
Telephone: 0191 551 5000   Fax: 0191 551 5125 Ticket Office
Registered in England: 69110

SUNDERLAND ASSOCIATION FOOTBALL CLUB LIMITED
Registered Office: Sunderland Stadium of Light Sunderland SR5 1SU
Telephone: 0191 551 5000 Fax: 0191 551 5125 Ticket Office: 0191 551 5151 Internet www.safc.com
Registered in England: 69116

Bring your family or friends to see Fulham or Boro for just £7.50 each!

As another New Year bonus for season ticket holders, we are giving your friends and family the opportunity to come and watch The Lads take on either **Fulham** or **Middlesbrough** at the Stadium of Light in January.

This is an excellent opportunity to bring along your son or daughter, husband or wife, or friends to a game of your choice.

These tickets are priced at a special rate of just £15 per pair, against the full price of up to £46 - a potential saving of £31! Your choice is the Fulham match on Saturday 19th January or the clash against Middlesbrough on Tuesday 29th January.

All you have to do is send is voucher number 58 and fill in the details on the application form enclosed, with a cheque for £15 or your credit card details, to **ST58 Offer, PO Box 165, Sunderland, SR5 1WF.** Alternatively you can apply in person at the SAFC Ticket Office. Once again, this offer is EXCLUSIVE to season ticket holders and tickets will be sold on a first come first served basis.

Why these offers?

Having reduced all season tickets prices this last year, we want to further repay your investment in the club by ensuring season ticket holders have priority access for extra tickets for the big games, and one-off special offers.

Separate application forms for both special offers are enclosed with this letter. Should you require further information, please call the Ticket Office on 0191 551 5151.

We would like to take this opportunity, on behalf of the players and the staff, to thank you for your invaluable support and wish you a very happy and prosperous New Year...lets hope it's a good one for the Red and White faithful.

Best wishes

Phil Clarkson
Ticket Office Manager

STLE UNITED
-OFF 1.00PM
OF LIGHT

OUT, YOU WILL BE
OU STATE OTHERWISE. YOU
L TRY TO ENSURE THAT THESE

£23.00 or £17.00

£17.00 or £8.00

nt left blank

JE NO.

UNDERLAND, SR5 1WF
O INCLUDE YOUR PAYMENT, A
R 59 AND THIS FORM.
T FEBRUARY 2002
RY 2002, YOUR APPLICATION HAS
DESTROYED.

ISU
Internet www.safc.com

F.T.M = Free Ticket Mackems.

Not since the mad days of their 'gold card' scheme in 1985 have they offered us so many free tickets!!!

Do you recall, when we were all in the Fulwell and Paddocks.

Have removed address and name and will remain anonymous... after all, we've got our tickets!!

JOKES

sunderland's first team squad have turned down Bob Murray's offer of an all expenses end of season break to Tenerife. Instead they want to go to Blackpool for a weekend so they can see what it's like to ride on an open top bus.

A Geordie, a Smogmonster and a Mackem all arrive at the Pearly gates together. St Peter informed them all that in order to gain entrance into heaven they would each have to answer one question. St Peter turned to the Geordie and asked, "What was the name of the ship that crashed into the iceberg? They made a movie about it."
The Geordie answered quickly "That would be the Titanic." So St Peter let him through the gate. St Peter then turned to the Smogmonster and not really wanting to let him and his chemical odours into heaven decided to ask a harder question. "How many people died on the ship?" Fortunately for him, the Smogmonster had just seen the movie and answered, "about 1,500."
"Well done that's right, you may enter," said St Peter who then turned to the Mackem and said, "Right ye prick, name them."

On the day that he sacked Howard Wilkinson, Bob Murray was gutted when he heard that Barry Sheene had died only minutes afterwards, as he could have helped sunderland turn the corner.

sunderland have moved quickly to halt rumours of a rift between Howard Wilkinson and Bob Murray after the chairman sacked the ex Mackem boss.
A club spokesman said, "It's ridiculous to suggest that there is a personality clash between the two, everyone at the club knows neither of them have a one.

If a Mackem and a Smogmonster both the same weight, height and age jumped from the top of the Eiffel tower in Paris on a warm sunny dry day in June, which one would hit the ground first? Who really gives a shit?

What do illegal immigrants and Kevin Phillips have in common?
England doesn't need them, as they have no use.

A Geordie, a Smogmonster and a Mackem are walking through the countryside when they see a sheep with its head stuck in a gate. Geordie says "I wish that was Britney Spears." The Smogmonster replied "No, I wish it was Naomi Campbell." The Mackem looked lovestruck and whispered "I wish it was Fucking dark."

Why do mackems plant potatoes round the edge of The Stadium of Light?
So that they have something to lift at the end of the season.

McCarthy signs an Ethnic Albanian for twenty-five quid from war torn Kosovo. On his debut he has a blinder and scores a hat trick in the last ten minutes. He can't wait to ring his folks back home. "Hello Mam, it's me I had a great game."
"Don't you talk to me about football, last night ten men beat your Dad up with baseball bats." He pleaded, "But Mam I scored. ."
She replied, "I don't care six men burst into the house this morning and dragged your sister into the street and gang raped her!!" "That's awful Mam but I did score 3 goals." "Goals, goals bloody goals the car's been torched and all our windows have been put through, the dog's been shot... And it's all your fault son!!"
"My fault Mam, how's it my fault?"
"Well we wanted to stay in Kosovo, but no you had to bring us to sunderland!!"

A Mackem fell asleep on the beach one day and the wind came up and blew sand all over him until he was covered with only his big toe sticking out. A Nympho was passing and saw his toe sticking up so pulled down her bikini bottom and squatted over the toe. She humped away until she was satisfied, pulled up her drawers and left.
The Mackem woke up, brushed himself down, not knowing what had happened. The next day his foot itched like hell and had a sore on it. He went to the Doctors and the Doctor told him he had Syphilis of the big toe.
"Syphilis of the big toe?" he inquired, isn't that rare." The Doctor said "Yes but if you think that's rare, I had a woman in here this morning with athlete's twat."

What's the difference between a Mackem and a Jet engine?
A Jet engine eventually stops whining.

Drug dealers in Pennywell, sunderland are supplying a new drug on the streets, Viagra eye drops. It does nothing for their sex life but it makes the Mackems look hard.

Burglars broke into the stadium of Light last night, but when asked, Bob Murray assured journalists that no cups had been pinched, as the thieves hadn't reached the canteen.

New Shirt Sponsor Revealed

SAFC and PAMPERS
P*ss up front & Sh*t at the back

Mick McCarthy was caught doing 150mph past the stadium of Light. In court the Judge fined him £175 but didn't endorse his licence stating that it had been a long time since anybody connected with safc had actually got 3 points in that area.

Steve Cram arrives at the main gates of St James Park to watch his beloved sunderland play their arch-rivals Newcastle United. He tries to gain entry to the hospitality suites, but is stopped by a 63 year old Newcastle steward who asks to see his ticket. "I must have left it in my car" explained Cram. The steward replied "Sorry sir but no ticket no entry!" Cram was furious "But mate I'm parked right across town at Manors Metro station." He continued shouting "Do you know who I am, I'm Steve Cram the 1,500 metres World Champion, the World record holder at the Mile and an Olympic gold medallist." The old bloke just looked at him and said "Well in that case it won't take you long ye Mackem twat."

What have Newcastle United, Middlesborough and sunderland all got in common?
Gates... Woodgate, Southgate and Relegate.

The next time you're having a bad day just imagine this. You're a Mackem Siamese twin, your brother is Gay and you are straight. But you both share the same arsehole! (Could be worse he could be a sunderland season ticket holder as well!)

In the 1992 F.A. Cup Final between Liverpool and sunderland, who was the last sunderland player to touch the ball in the match?
Clue; It was in the first half.

What's the difference between Santa Claus and a Mackem in the San Siro?
One doesn't exist and never will and the other one has a big white beard wears a red suit and rides on a sleigh pulled by reindeers.

The Post Office has just recalled their latest stamps. They had pictures of the sunderland players on them and the public

What is sunderland famous for?

A: It's Cathedral   B: Nowt

C: It's Illuminations   D: International Airport

were spitting on the non-sticky side.

sunderland fans - don't go wasting money on another replica team shirt this summer. Simply strap a large penis to your forehead and it will be quite obvious to everybody, which team you support.

BBC STATEMENT. We have received thousands of complaints from Wearside over the years complaining of Pro Newcastle and Anti-Mackem content in various TV programmes such as The Likely Lads, Auf Wiedersehn Pet, Spender, Crocodile Shoes, Grafters, Byker Grove and Our Friends in the North, as well as a host of Ant and Dec programmes to name but a few. In response that there aren't enough programmes involving Mackems and the city of sunderland, the BBC will now be showing Crimewatch three times a week as well as extended episodes of Kilroy.

What's the difference between a Northumbria Water lorry and Mickey Gray's schoolteacher?
One's a water tanker and the other taught a...

Quasimodo asks Esmerelda if he really is the most ugly man alive. Esmeralda says, "Go upstairs and ask the magic mirror who is the ugliest of them all and the mirror will tell you." Five minutes later Quasie comes down the stairs crying and asks Esmerelda, "Who the fuck are Peter Reid and Stephen Wright?

SUNDERLAND
ASSOCIATION FOOTBALL CLUB

To All Stewards

Complimentary Tickets

It has been agreed by the Board as a "one off thank you" for all the stewards excellent work this season to allocate each steward 2 complimentary tickets for one of the following three matches.

Bolton Wanderers
Southampton
Leicester City

These tickets cannot be resold and are only for immediate family use.

If you wish to participate please complete below and return to Safety Officer as soon as possible

JOHN DAVIDSON
08/02/02

JOKES

THE AULD ONES ARE THE BEST

What's the difference between a triangle and sunderland football team?
A triangle has got 3 points...

What do you have if you have a thousand Mackems buried up to their necks in sand?
Not enough sand!

Heard about the Mackem tap dancer?
He fell in the sink.

What's safc and a teabag got in common?
Neither ever stays in the cup long.

Why do Mackems never get piles?
Because God made them perfect arseholes.

Experts are predicting that sunderland will stay in the premiership for at least one more season... Spring.

When Peter Reid was manager of sunderland he asked Sir Bobby how Newcastle had such a good team. Bobby told him it all stemmed from the training pitch and told Peter to set eleven dustbins out on the pitch as opposition and practice set pieces and game plans in a real match situation. Reidy thought it was a great idea and thanked Sir Bobby for his help. A couple of weeks later Bobby bumped into Peter Reid and asked, "So how did the training with the dustbins go then?" Reid replied, "Not too bad, we only got beat 4-2!!"

Mick McCarthy fainted in a building society and when he woke up he asked, "Where am I," A member of staff replied, "You're in the Alliance," to which McCarthy moaned, "What happened to the second and third divisions and the Conference?"

What do you say to a Mackem with a job?
"Can I have a Big Mac?"

What do you call a Mackem in a Three Bedroom Semi?
A Burglar.

A Wigan supporter arrives at sunderland's very small railway station for their match against the Mackems, but hasn't got a clue on how to get to the Stadium of Light? So he asks an old lady, "excuse me pet, but do you know the way to the football ground?" She says "It's easy just follow the crowds son." Twenty minutes later he ended up in Woolworth's!!

Why do Mackem's carry shit in their wallets?
For identification purposes.

Why do mackems smell so bad?
So that Blind people can hate them as well.

Why wasn't Christ born in sunderland?
Because they couldn't find three wise men and a virgin

Why did Mrs Hesford climb on top?
Because he always fucked up!

What's Black and Brown, and looks great on a Mackem?
A Doberman Dog.

Attendances on Wearside have always been well below that of their Big City neighbours Newcastle United. Listed below are a few examples picked at random from throughout history of the two clubs' average league attendances. On some occasions the attendance at Newcastle is more than double than the ones at sunderland.

AVERAGE ATTENDANCES OVER A FULL LEAGUE SEASON

Season	Newcastle United	sunderland	Difference
1907/08	27,875	17,470	- 10,405
1909/10	24,825	11,615	- 13,210
1911/12	24,995	12,555	- 12,440
1926/27	36,510	18,142	- 18,368
1932/33	25,992	17,254	- 8,738
1946/47	49,379	35,301	- 14,078
1959/60	36,037	22,831	- 13,206
1969/70	37,553	21,790	- 15,763
1970/71	29,735	15,780	- 13,955
1973/74	32,861	24,409	- 8,452
1983/84	29,811	16,180	- 13,631
1986/87	24,792	13,601	- 11,191
1992/93	29,018	17,258	- 11,760
1993/94	33,679	16,934	- 16,745
1994/95	34,690	15,344	- 19,346

These days St James Park is full to capacity (Over 52,000) for every league match unless the visiting club have a few empty seats. Any returned tickets are snapped up by Newcastle fans. Yet 'The Stadium of Light' (48,000 allegedly?) is never full even when they play Nufc, as there's thousands of empty seats.

R.I.P

You went to Wembley Stadium
Your money you did pay
March nineteen hundred and eighty five
On a wet and windy day
You showed them how to sing
And you showed them how to sup
The only thing you didn't do was win the Fucking Cup

The fans they went in thousands
Singing all the way
They came by bus and train load
So happy and so Gay
The first half ended boringly
The second not so droll
The Norwich end erupted
When Chisholm scored the goal

The ball it came to Venison
He ran towards the goal
Van Wyk he slid and handled
The Roker roar was bold
Up stepped Little Walker
Ready for the punt
He took the shot and blew the lot
He'd missed (the stupid cunt)

No more goals did follow
The game it died a death
The best part of the match to come
was the whistle by the ref.

The mackems then went up the steps
Oh how the players cried
We'll not forget the magic day
When fucking sunderland died

IT'S A FACT

Struggling to score goals, sunderland's Howard Wilkinson bought a 3rd choice keeper for the same money as Man. City paid for England striker Robbie Fowler.

NUFC scored more goals in 14 Champions League matches against the likes of Juventus, Inter Milan, Leverkusen, Feyenoord & Barcelona than the mackems did in 38 league matches.

NUFC won more matches in 14 Champions League matches than sunderland did in 38 league ones.

Status Quo opened the SOL with the song 'Rocking all over the world', another of their big hits is 'Down, Down'.

Cheesy Chips is the Mackem favourite for Sunday lunch.

Sewpa Kev relegated twice with two different clubs.

With four months of 2002/03 season left to go, SAFC couldn't mathematically catch NUFC.

Wouldn't let the fans out at half-time in Charlton match.

Sugar Puffs sales hit an all-time low on Wearside when Kevin Keegan advertised them.

Sunderland scored three own goals at home to Charlton Athletic.

Even with the help of over 2,000 Geordies sunderland still couldn't sell out their crucial play-off match with Gillingham.

Kevin Phillips - 30 goals? 20 goals? Not even double figures this season - it's a fact, he doesn't score goals.

Semi-final of Worthington Cup - sunderland v Leicester, mackems had 10,000 empty seats even though Leicester brought 8,000.

NUFC were last team to win Tyne/Wear derby at Roker Park.

NUFC were first team to win a Tyne/Wear derby at Stadium of Light.

The Yorkshire Ripper hoaxer who wasted thousands of hours of Police time had a Mackem accent.

The foot & mouth epidemic was allegedly started by a Mackem.

SAFC give kids cheap tickets.

SAFC give the kids' parents cheap tickets.

SAFC give students cheap tickets.

SAFC give the elderly cheap tickets.

Don Hutchison kissed the sunderland badge at St.James Park in front of 50,000 Geordies, days later he left sunderland.

Niall Quinn gave all his testimonial money to charity. To qualify for a testimonial it's the standard to serve at least ten years, Quinn was nowhere near that.

sunderland Qualify for Europe

The village of sunderland was today celebrating when it was announced that European soccer is returning to Roker Park for the first time since that horrible day back in 1973 when that man dressed as a tramp ran across the field in London. At first they tried to get into Europe by entering The Eurovision Song Contest when the whole of the first team sang a song about Wearside, Cher's classic "Gypsies, Tramps and Thieves," but were well beaten by Brotherhood of Man.

But the Northumberland and District F.A today revealed that the mackems form over the past few seasons has been so poor that they've had no choice but to make room for them in the 1994 Grace Darling Coastline Cup. At first there was doubt over whether sunderland's geographical position would prevent them from entering the Coastline Cup, but as their chairman was quick to point out: "This doesn't really matter as we are called sunderland F.C., yet Stadium of Light is nowhere near sunderland centre. In fact we're nearer the coastline." He continued "This is great news for our fans and everybody involved, just the lift we've needed and I'm sure we can re-create the magic of those great European nights enjoyed over the years by Celtic, Liverpool, Rangers and of course Newcastle United."

Sunderland have been drawn in Group B along with Amble, Holy Island, The Farne Islands and the might of the North East coast, St Mary's Lighthouse. Each club play each other at home and away with the winners of each group playing for the Coastline Cup at The feathers Caravan Site, Whitley Bay, in the final.

Other clubs aren't so excited about sunderland's entry into Europe. Farne Islands Athletics boss told us that they've got thousands of birds on the island, so there's already enough shite on the pitch even before the mackems arrive. Seahouses police have warned Wearside fans that there will be no alcohol allowed on the Grace Darling rowing boat for the trip abroad to the Farne Islands. Also fans are advised to check the local press for safe crossing times when playing away to Holy Island and St Mary's Lighthouse. The first away match is away to amble and sunderland's manager is confident. "Yes, of course it's going to be difficult, European ties always are, but we've a strong squad and we've got to be confident and go there and hopefully hold on for a goal-less draw!" Amble's manager yellow coat Ted Fatman, is quietly confident. "We stand a good chance, it depends on who's staying at the caravan site this year and how many prefer a game of football opposed to a shopping trip o Alnwick Market. But as long as we can field eleven players, preferably men, I'm sure we will have no problems."

The feeling is though, that sunderland's hardest test could be the trip to Holy Island, as the monks have been preparing for this one, training daily, losing hair and eating Bachelor's Soup. But the Wearsiders better watch out as the Monks haven't had a shag for thousands of years and the sight of eleven fannies running around in red & white stripes could cause some pelvic movement amongst the Holy Island team. It looks as though they could bring different meaning to the phrase: "Back passage to Europe."

JOKES

Q: What do Mackems and beer bottles have in common?
A: They're both empty from the waist up.

Q: What does a Mackem girl say after having sex?
A: Do you all play for the same team?

Q: Why do lasses from sunderland wear knickers?
A: To keep their ankles warm.

Q: What do you throw a mackem when he is drowning?
A: His wife and kids.

Q: What's the difference between safc and a toothpick?
A: A toothpick has more points.

It has just come to light that when Bob Stokoe was manager of sunderland he fined two of his players, after it was discovered that they had broken club rules by having sex, the night before the 1973 Cup Final. The club confirmed that the fines would have been heavier if a woman had been involved.

Q: What is the difference between a Catfish and a sunderland fan?
A: One is an ugly, scum, sucking, bottom-feeder and the other is a fish.

Did you hear about the Gay Mackem with a cock like a rocket?
His boyfriend is over the moon.

Top Sportswear company's Nike, Adidas and Lonsdale are battling it out to seal a mega-sponsorship deal with sunderland boxer Billy Hardy, in time for his next fight. Billy's promoter revealed that it's amazing how much cash is being offered to advertise on the sole of his boots.

What do you call a Mackem at a European football match?
A neutral supporter.

What do you call a Mackem at Old Trafford?
The ref.

What do you call a Mackem at Anfield?
A dreamer.

A little Mackem asks his dad how many points Sunderland have. His dad looks at his son and says proudly "Fifteen son, we've got Fifteen." "So where is my Easter Egg then Dad?" asks the kid.

Three pregnant women (A Geordie, a Mackem and an African) are totally devastated when their newborn baby boys get mixed up in the maternity Ward. The Nurses are so embarrassed, but decide to sort it out and ask the Dads to choose their child. The Geordie gets first pick of the bunch, "Give me the black one just to be on the safe side."

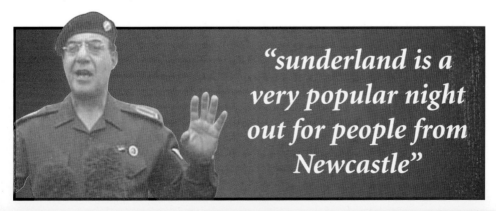

"sunderland is a very popular night out for people from Newcastle"

LET'S ALL LAUGH AT SUNDERLAND   23

Three Mackems go for a job on a building site. The first one from Hendon goes in the Gaffer's office and is told that if he answers one question he's got the job. Gaffer asks, "What's three plus three plus three," One hundred and six," replied the mackem. Next was the second Mackem from Pennywell. The Gaffer asks the same question again "What's three plus three plus three," after a couple of minutes the Mackem replies "Wednesday." The Gaffer is furious and chases the thick arsehole out and invites the last Mackem in. "Are you any good at very simple arithmetic?" he asks the Mackem from Downhill. The Mackem nods and is told that if he answers the question correctly he's got the job. Once again the Gaffer asks "What's three plus three plus three," After 15 minutes the Mackem eventually replies "Nine."
A relieved Gaffer is overjoyed, "Well done, that's correct and the job's yours, but can I just ask how you came to that answer." The Mackem looking pleased with himself replied " Simple I just took one hundred and six away from Wednesday!"

Why are there no lifts at the Stadium of light? (Not Benfica's Ground but sunderland's)
Because they are sick of the voice saying 'Going down.'

Did you hear about the kid who asked for a cowboy outfit for Christmas and his Mam and Dad bought him a sunderland strip.

An American visits the north-east on vacation and being a sports fanatic he wants to visit the region's Soccer stadiums. He watches Boro at the Riverside then he visits St James Park to watch Newcastle United. At half time he gets talking to a group of Geordies and asks them where sunderlando is. The Geordies reply, "Do you not mean sunderland," No said the Yank "sunderlando." The Geordies explained, "There's no such place mate" Well said the American "Every time I look at the English soccer results I see Burnley 2 sunderland0, sunderland0 Derby 1, sunderland0 Wigan 3."

A Mackem says to his wife "My Olympic condoms have arrived darling, so tonight I'm going to wear a Gold one." His wife replied, "Why don't you wear the Silver one and come second for a change!!"

A Geordie living in sunderland is dying of a rare bone disease. His son asks "Dad why are you telling the neighbours you're dying of Aids?" The Dad looks at his son and holding his hand says "So that none of these Mackem twats shag your mam when I'm dead."

Did you hear about the Mackem who studied five days for a Urine Test?

Q. What do you call a Mackem girl's cleavage?
A. Silicon Valley!

Q: How did the Mackem find his sister in the woods?
A: Just Fine!!

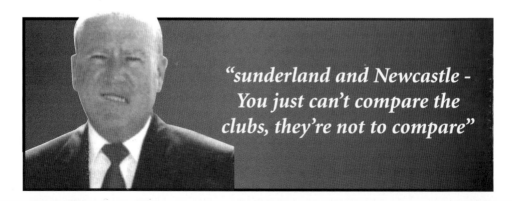

"sunderland and Newcastle - You just can't compare the clubs, they're not to compare"

Q: What do you call a Mackem with one O' Level?
A: Top of the class.

Mackem says to Geordie "I've seen all the Star Trek films and episodes on television, featuring Chinese, Blacks, Scottish, American, Irish and even Vulcans, yet I've never seen any Mackems?" Geordie reply's "That's because it's set in the future ye thick bastard."

A Mackem goes for his weekly shop at Tesco's and is emptying the contents of his trolley at the checkout. On to the conveyor belt he puts a bottle of Whiskey, 24 cans of Lager, 12 cans of Guinness, 7 Frozen Pizza's, 4 microwave curries, 7 Pot Noodles, 36 Bags of crisps, 6 Mars Bars, 7 frozen meals for one, 2 packets of biscuits, FHM Magazine and 40 tabs!! The girl on the checkout looks at him and says, "I can tell you live on your own." The bloke looks amazed, "How do you know that?" The girl replies, "Because you're a right ugly Twat."

A young Mackem asked his Mam, "I thought you said you were washing my red and white football top." "I have" replied his Mam "Well what's it doing in the middle of the back garden" said the young lad. His Mam shouted angrily "I'll kill the thieving bastards, they've stole my pegs again!"

The Wearside church of England association inform us that the most common form of wedding proposal in their area is: "You're what?"

What would you like for Christmas the Mackem parents asked their young son. "I wanna watch," he said. So they let him.

Wearside boxer Billy Hardy used to fight under the name of Rembrandt, because he was always on the canvas!

I see they've cleaned the River Wear up. You can get Salmon in the Wear now, I've seen them floating in their tins.

Two Newcastle fans travel down to Mackemland for the match against sunderland. They arrange to meet some other Geordies at the B&Q car park but have trouble finding it, so they stop a couple of locals wearing red and white scarves and ask. "Can you help us lads, is there a B&Q in sunderland?" The two Mackem's look at each other totally puzzled before one says, "An S and a U and a N, D, E, R, and L, A, N, D, eh no I don't think so mate."

What do you get when you offer a sunderland fan a penny for his thoughts? Change!

A Mackem goes to Blackpool with his lass and visits a sex shop. She asks the man behind the counter for a vibrator. "What colour would you like, we've got Red ones, Green ones, Flesh coloured ones or Black ones?" "What about the Tartan one" she asked. "That's my fucking Flask ye filthy cow!!"

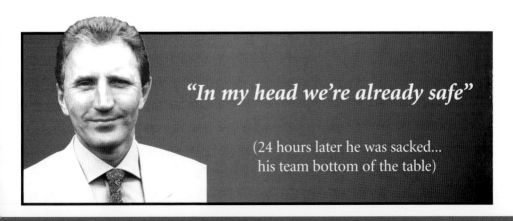

"In my head we're already safe"

(24 hours later he was sacked... his team bottom of the table)

sunderland fade and die

To the tune of American Pie

Written by M.Edmondson 2003

A long, long time ago
The mackems still remember
How that monkey used to make them smile
But Peter Reid he blew his chance
He led the mackems a merry dance
And sunderland are still stuck with Kevin Kyle

But Bob Murray had a masterstroke
He brought in Wilko, what a joke
Not a penny in the bank
First team not worth a wank

Next they got plastic Irishman
Mick McCarthy – Roy Keane's not a fan
Us Geordies laughed coz they're down the pan
Whilst on the drink in Milan

CHORUS
So bye bye watch the sad mackems cry
Lose all the players
And their money from Sky
And Geordie Boys drinking champagne and rye
Watching sunderland fade and die
sunderland fade and die

Verse 2

Have you been to the San Siro
The Nou Camp twice, Kiev and Rome
You Know deep down you'll never go
I bet you know the way to Ashton Gate
You were in the third in '88'
We were there when Cascarino sealed you fate

Well I know that you'll get beat by Crewe
When the Toon are winning at Man U,
Walsall, Wigan and other shite
Will be playing at the stadium of light

It'll be a long time before we play you again
Phillips long gone, we'll beat you by ten
We'll be champions of Europe by then
The day that sunderland died

(Repeat chorus)

Verse 3

You live in a town but call it a city
No Cathedral and the Bridges is shitty
The glass centres your pride and joy
You think ye posh eating chips and cheese
Ye talk deed funny Weez Keez are theeze
You're so jealous of Newcastle and it shows

When you go on holiday ye fly from the Toon
Vaux Breweries shut now ye drinking broon
You all live on the wear
All mackem boys queer
Kids and students get in for free
They used to go to see the chimpanzee
Next season they'll just watch ITV
The day that sunderland died

(Repeat chorus)

JAMIE RILEY BOOKMAKERS

Fancy a flutter on the 2003/04 Season?

Champions League: **Real Madrid 3-1, Man Utd 5-1, Juventus 7-1, Ajax 12-1, Newcastle United 14-1**

Premier League: **Arsenal 5-2, Newcastle United 4-1, Man Utd 6-1, Liverpool 8-1, Chelsea 12-1**

F.A. Cup: **Newcastle United 3-1, Arsenal 7-2, Spurs 5-1, Man Utd 6-1, Everton 10-1**

First Division: **Norwich 2-1, Derby 11-2, West Brom 6-1, Wigan 10-1, Ipswich 12-1, sunderland 200-1**

Autoglass Trophy: **Hartlepool 6-1, Yeovil 10-1, York 14-1, sunderland 33-1**

First manager to be sacked:	Kevin Ball (sunderland) 7-1
First manager to run away:	Mick McCarthy (sunderland) - Evens
First club to go bust:	sunderland - Evens
Most unluckiest team award:	sunderland - Betting Suspended

MICK McCARTHY JOKES

Mick McCarthy has made a new signing. He has signed Frankie Dettori as he thinks that it's the only way they will win the next DERBY.

Mick McCarthy bumps into Kevin Phillips in the Butchers and asks him why he's not at training, Phillips replies "I'm getting a pound of sausages and half a pound of Black Pudding Gaffer!" McCarthy goes mad, telling him to get to training and he would collect his order. As McCarthy leaves the Butchers shop he bumps into Bobby Robson, "What you doing down this neck of the woods" asks Bobby, to which McCarthy replies "Hello Bobby, I've just been getting a pound of sausages and half a pound of Black Pudding for Kevin Phillips." Bobby says "Hey Mick you've got one hell of a deal there!"

Did you hear what Saddam said to Bin Ladin?
I wouldn't like to be in Mick McCarthy's shoes!

Mick McCarthy is set to sign two Dutch internationals this week, Hertz Van Hire and his brother Avis.

Mick McCarthy has swooped to sign Scottish pair Ben Dover and Phil McCracken!

Mick McCarthy calls Mickey Gray into his office and lays his cards on the table. "Look Mickey you started your career as a Left winger, then dropped into Left Midfield. When I arrived at the club your position was Left Back, so just to let you know that I've been watching the situation and next week you will be left out."

Mick McCarthy had just taken over as manager of bottom of the table sunderland and they were playing away to fellow strugglers West Ham. Before the match they stopped off for a pre-match meal at a hotel in London. The waitress approached McCarthy and asked him what he would like off the a la carte menu, to which he replied "I'd like a Steak Diane please." "How would you like your Steak sir?" asked the waitress. McCarthy said "Medium to well done please." The waitress continued "And what about the vegetables sir," McCarthy replied "Oh just give them eleven plates of chips!!"

A group of tourists are on the top deck of a bus touring Newcastle City centre when

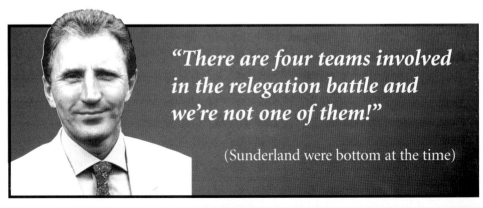

"There are four teams involved in the relegation battle and we're not one of them!"

(Sunderland were bottom at the time)

the tour guide asks if anybody would like to tell a joke. A bloke from Leeds stood up and said, "I know a Mackem joke," but a bloke protested from the back seat, "No don't, I'm a sunderland fan." The tour guide looked at him and said, "Don't worry we will explain it afterwards."

Mick McCarthy signs an unknown Japanese player for sunderland. Before his first training session McCarthy goes over tactics with a piece of chalk on the blackboard. He firstly drew a set of goal posts; "G-O-A-L" he spelt out. Then he drew a round object and spelled out the word B-A-L-L. He then explained that the B-A-L-L had to go in the G-O-A-L. A bit bemused by it all the Japanese player turned to his boss and told him in broken English, "I told you when I signed I understood the English language. McCarthy replied, "It's not you I'm talking too, it's the rest of the useless buggers!"

A reporter is interviewing Mick McCarthy and Gary Megson. He first asks Mick what his long term plans for sunderland are? "Well, I see us becoming a good average first division team, who will win as many as we lose and finish in the top half of the league." The reporter then puts the same question to Gary of West Brom, who answers, "I think that, now we have been relegated, we will be able to mount a successful challenge to win the first Division title. Once we're back up in the Premier League we can win the title at the first attempt then, we will carry off the European cup for the next 5 years." "Don't you think that's a little bit over-optimistic, Gary?" asks the interviewer, to which Gary replies, "Well, Mick started it."

Bobby Robson, Steve McClarren and Mick McCarthy visited the Angel of the North. They all decided to ask it questions about their clubs. Bobby says "When will Newcastle United next win a major trophy?" the Angel replied "I guarantee they will finally win a Trophy next season, and then go on to be the best team in the land, for years to come." "Great!" replies Bobby. Steve steps up and asks, "Will Boro ever win anything?" "Well..." says the Angel, "I can't guarantee they will win anything when you're around." "Bloody hell, nothing goes my way!" Screamed Steve. Finally Mick steps up and confidently asks the same question, the Angel whispers in to Mick's ear, "Come back tomorrow on your own and I'll give you a hint on what's wrong." So the next day Mick McCarthy returns and the Angel says, "Well I'll get to the point first of all you've got Thomas Sorensen in goal (10 minutes later). . . and finally you've got Kevin Phillips partnering Tore Andre Flo up front. Basically you've got a team full of retarded Mackems. Oh, Yes... and if you want to be at a winning club, I heard there's a position as a Turnstile operator at St James Park!"

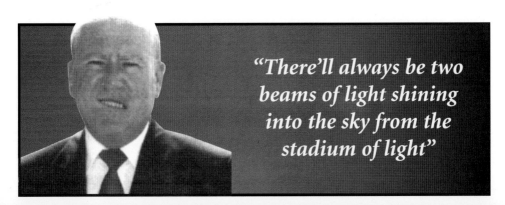

"There'll always be two beams of light shining into the sky from the stadium of light"

JOKES

A Mackem goes to Blackpool with his lass and visits a sex shop. She asks the man behind the counter for a vibrator. "What colour would you like, we've got Blue ones, Green ones, Flesh coloured ones or Black ones?" "What about that red one behind you" she asked. "That's the fucking fire extinguisher ye dirty cow!!"

A young lad announced to his mate that he had a bedroom full of footballs, which he'd collected from every Premiership ground. His mate was impressed but said he could identify where each ball had come from just by smelling and touching them. He picked up the first ball and gave it a good feel, then smelt it, "This one's from Middlesborough because I can smell the chemicals on it and see that it has been hoofed about the pitch." The lad was impressed and threw him the second ball, "Oh yes, without a doubt my favourite it's from Newcastle, as I can smell the breweries and can see that it has been kicked around gracefully." Again he was spot on with his answer so the lad threw him the third ball, "Without a doubt this one's from sunderland" he said immediately. The boy was confused "But you haven't even smelt it," "I don't need to, I can feel it's going down!"

Two Mackems are walking down Northumberland Street when one of them spots a sign in a shop window. It reads Shirts-50p, Trousers-£1, Suits £2. "Here" says the first Mackem "have you seen that, Shirts 50p, Trousers £1 and Suits only £2. It looks like a real bargain, why don't we go

Trampwatch

Mags beware, having failed to fill the stadium of shite by kidnapping every kid from the Tees to the Tweed, Murray and F***ling have turned their attention to the coffin dodgers in care homes.

As the letter below shows, the mackem equivalent to Burke and Hare will stop at nothing.

Johna

Tel: 01670 819 277 Fax: 01670 819 255
Northern Divisional Office, Moorhouse Farm, Moorhouse Lane
Ashington, Northumberland, NE63 9LJ

Highfield Holdings

Memo

To: Care Home Managers
From: Sarah Hall
CC: Clare Savage, Louise Gibson, Rosalind Winch
Date: 28 January 2003
Re: Sunderland Stadium of Light – Day Trips

Once again, NHP have offered all care homes the chance to see Sunderland Football Club play two home matches, the first being on 22nd February 2003 playing against Middlesbrough and the second on 15th March 2003 playing against Bolton. On the day a corporate bar service will be available with reduced priced beverages and a padded executive outside to watch the game. All transport will be paid for by NHP and arranged between myself and individual care homes.

Unfortunately the Sunderland vs. Middlesbrough game (22/02) does not have any availability for wheelchair users, but the second game Sunderland vs. Bolton (15/3) has plenty. The dress code for the match is casual, but everyone is advised to 'wrap up warm'!

Bill Colvin has also asked that Manager's personally invite NCSC Inspectors, Care Managers, Social Workers, etc, along to the game – this being an excellent way to promote the care homes.

Could you all please get names of residents, whether they use a wheelchair, staff names, guest names, which game you would like to attend, or both, to me as soon as possible so we can book the tickets and start arranging transport.

Should you have any queries please call. Thanks.

Kind regards,

Sarah Hall

in and buy the lot and take them back to sunderland and sell them on and make a profit." "Aye, that's a great idea but there's one problem though, they won't serve us because when the lady in the shop hears our accents she'll know we're Mackems." "Don't worry about that" says the first Mackem, I went to school with a Geordie and I've got the accent off to a tee." So both the Mackems walk into the shop and ask the lady if the sign in the window is correct. "What do you mean," she says. Ye Knaa "Shirts 50p, Trousers £1 and Suits only £2, and we want to buy the lot" said the first Mackem. The lady looked at them and smiled "You're both Mackems aren't you." The two Mackems are totally shocked, "How did you know that like?" they gasped. Because you're in a Dry Cleaners ye thick twats!!!"

A Mackem pegs it and goes to hell. The Devil says that there is only one room left and shows him in. When he opens the door all these Mancs are standing up to their waists in shite. Oh well, it will just have to do thinks the Mackem. Half an hour later the Devil opens the door and says "Right lads, tea-breaks over now back on your heads!!"

When Mick Buxton was manager of sunderland he tried to sign female singer Marti Caine as he thought she would fit in well with his team, as she had nothing up front.

A man is walking through a park in Newcastle one day when he hears a child screaming. To his horror he sees a Rottweiller dog attacking a small boy. Without a second thought the man dives onto the dog and a monumental battle takes place. The man gets bitten and clawed to within an inch of his life but somehow manages to pull the dog off the young boy and with his last ounce of strength just manages to strangle the ferocious beast. A man with a camera rushes over to the bloody scene. "I'm a reporter from the local paper and that is the bravest deed I have ever seen, I can just see the headlines now 'GEORDIE HERO SAVES CHILD FROM CERTAIN DEATH' "That's very kind of you replies the hero, but I'm not a Geordie, I'm a Mackem" The reporter tells him it's not a problem and so the headlines that evening read 'MACKEM BASTARD KILLS FAMILY PET.'

The Mackem Robin Hood has retired, as the last coach he held up was full of Newcastle fans.

Michael Barrymore has just signed for sunderland and says he is really looking forward to having ten arseholes playing about in front of him and ten thousand pricks behind him.

Do you know how to save a drowning Mackem?
No? ...Good.

sunderland are looking forward to their next three points at St. James Park... against Exeter City.

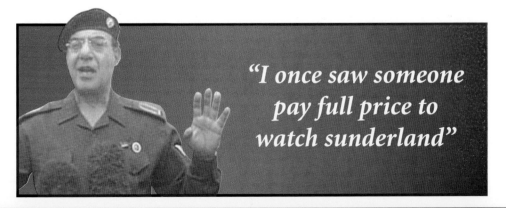

"I once saw someone pay full price to watch sunderland"

DIARY OF A 'ROCK ARD' MACKEM HOOLIGAN

Aug 16th home to Burnley. Hundreds of Burnley fans expected up for the first match of the season. Unfortunately still on holiday at Crimdon Dean.

Aug 23rd Gillingham away. I hate those cockney bastards! I it wasn't for the fact I had to unpack and watch Coronation Street I swear I would have been there.

Aug 30th Preston North End at home. They've only got a small hardcore following so I decided to make an appearance, turning up at Seaburn station wearing my Pringle jumper, Farah pants and Winners two-stripe orange trainers. The Preston Inter City Firm never showed, obviously soft as shite.

Sep 7th Crystal Palace away. How far?

Sep 14th Norwich at Stadium Of Light. Decided to miss it as we lost our previous four matches.

Sep 21st Cup fever hits Wearside as Yeovil Town arrive for the Autoglass Trophy, went to see the sunderland lights with our lass.

Sep 24th Millwall away, the big one. Really up for it, hope it's on Tyne Tees.

Oct 11th Queens Park Rangers in the Worthington Cup, there's no way I'm going to risk my life in Glasgow as those Jocks are mad.

Oct 18th Stoke away. No chance, must start saving for Xmas.

Oct 25th Walsall at home, kicked off in the chip shop. We chased two of their boys through the Bridges shopping centre, they were last seen in the safety of the soft play area at Crowtree leisure centre.

Nov 15th Watford at home, nearly got arrested. I was standing next to the away end chanting 'we hate cockneys' and if the copper hadn't come over and told me to shut up, I'd have been over the fence and stuck into the Watford headhunters, especially the woman wearing specs.

Dec 6th Wimbledon away. Got pissed on slimfast and Babycham & sang 'Have you ever seen a Geordie in Milton Keyneseo?'.

Dec 13th Rotherham at home. Still hungover, must have been one of those cherries in my Babycham.

Dec 26th Boxing Day at Reading. I think I'll read my new annuals, 'Jackie' and 'Scorcher'. Rode my new bike to the Stadium Of Light, only fell off six times – god knows how many times it would have been if it had only two wheels.

Jan 1st FA Cup 3rd round, Leeds away. Unbeaten all year, thinking about taking stabilisers off my bike. Got a ticket off my uncle who lives in Yorkshire. Leeds and us go back a long way to Wembley '63 when Jim Montgomery scored a hat-trick and Malcolm MacDonald never had a sniff.

Feb 7th After missing the last six weeks through injury we were drawn away to Newcastle in the Cup, twenty of us piled into the back of a Transit van on the Saturday morning, full of drink, and headed for the Lake District.

Feb 14th Home to Derby. Got a brand new brolly for Valentine's off Cyril, couldn't wait to try it out. On the day of the match we were chased by a gang of Derby but lost them both when the fifteen of us split up. It never rained.

Mar 17th I just love Wednesday matches, West Brom the visitors. I arrived just in time for the 3pm kick-off and found the gates locked. Obviously another sell-out.

Mar 27th Wolves at the Stadium Of Light. I never miss a match, the atmosphere was brilliant – twenty thousand in the ground, mostly wearing gold & black – must be our new away kit. I nearly spilt my half of lager & lime when we went one up, good old Paul Ince – when did we sign him?

Apr 10th Stoke City at home, I've never seen so many red & white stripes in my life in the Metro FM stand – sunderland are back. We're too good to go down and have just been unlucky, again. Just hope Kevin Kyle can stay fit and get his first goal.

Apr 11th Weather has improved so it's back to the caravan at Crimdon Dean.

And some news just in...

Six thousand cases of imported frozen Cheesy Chips were stolen from sunderland Docks today. A Police spokesman said "It would have taken at least four hours for an organised criminal gang to do this." A spokesman for the Mackem Dockers said, "Whatever happens when we are on our tea break is none of our concern."

"Police in southwick, sunderland are clamping down on local dealers who make fortunes selling stolen cars which have been sawn in half and welded to other vechicles" said Chief Superintendent Barlow, from the wheel of his E-type, Combine Harvester.

Scientists have cloned an Octopus with a Mackem! It's a right ugly Bastard but you want to see the Fucker eat its Cheesy Chips at 11 o'clock on a Saturday night!

BREAKING NEWS; Two Thousand Troops from the Mackem Light Infantry have entered Jordan on the Iraqi border. A British war official has reported that all the men have returned safely without loss, but Jordan has a hell of a sore fanny.

Blackburn striker Dwight Yorke the father of Jordan's child, is set to join sunderland when the transfer window opens, as he wants to play with even bigger tits.

Geordie Steinberg came back from holiday in Jerusalem. His father asked if he had managed to pray at the Wailing Wall. "Sorry fatha" he says "I couldn't get near the bugger for all the Mackems."

A Mackem couple from the Barnes area of sunderland were in court today charged with indecent exposure and behaviour, when they were caught having sex earlier this year next to Becher's Brook at Aintree racecourse. They've asked for another 12 fences to be taken into consideration.

Bob Murray has just announced that sunderland are to play their football at the bottom of the Sea from next season, as there's 20,000 leagues down there and he hopes he can win one of them.

The Police also revealed that vandals today had smashed the toilets at Hendon Police Station. When asked about the damage the Chief Inspector said he was saddened and hoped to catch the culprits, but he had nothing to go on at the moment!!

Some tragic news just in, that a coach full of sunderland fans travelling to their match against Gillingham has skidded off the M25 just south of the Dartford Crossing. Fireman are still trying to get the new '52 Seat Coach' out of the wreckage. More news when we get it.

F*** OFF P

(To the tune of Da

You'll be crying in your beer
All you sad twats on the Wear
In six months time, you'll be sick as f***
Getting beat by Coventry
Getting stuffed at Highbury
And all because your Gaffa's a chimpanzee

CHORUS 1
Fuck off Peter Reid
Oh what can it mean?
To a sad mackem Bastard
And a shit football team

My nana once saw you
In a cage at Chester zoo
Now you're a hairy red & white baboon
You'll never see the day that Europe comes your way
And never get 3 points off the Toon

CHORUS 2
Fuck off Monkeys Heed
You're so f***ing mean?
You're a sad mackem Bastard
With a shit football team

(Repeat first chorus to fade)

ETER REID
(ydream Believer)

T.O.S.S.A.R

The Old Shitty Sleetproof Anorak Retailers

New to our range of nostalgic football workwear is the classic multi purpose '1973 Stokoe Wembley Raincoat' as seen below, worn by the legendary Bob Stokoe.

The Multi purpose

'73 Wembley Raincoat'
'87 Relegation Bench coat'

ONLY
£32.99

Reversible

The Raincoat is also worn by Bong-eyed Detective Columbo on T.V, and comes with a Tossar lifetime guarantee, or your money back.

The coat is multi purpose and can be turned inside out, as proved 14 Years later by Bob Stokoe in May 1987, when he wore the same coat and helped steer sunderland out of the Second Division and into the Third!! Look like a tramp and wear;

'The STOKOE 87 RELEGATION BENCH COAT.'

SIEMEN *Stains*   HARDY VEG   SIEMEN *Stains*

Stare Into The Picture

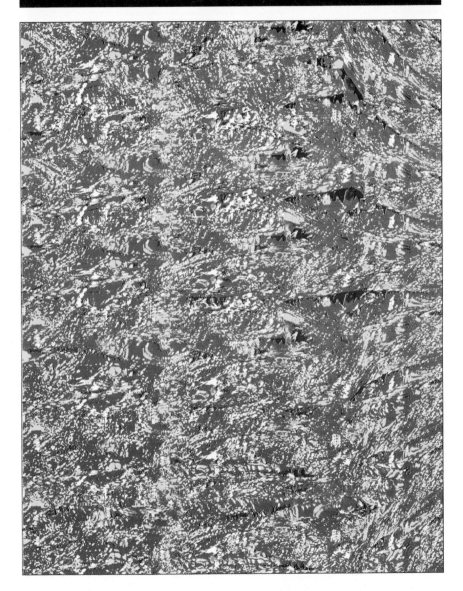

sunderland playing in The Premiership
(Can You See It? - No, Neither Can I)

And some news just in...

Saddam Hussein was on TV last night saying "To prove I'm still alive sunderland played shite on Saturday and got a well deserved stuffing." George Bush and Tony Blair said that it could have been recorded at anytime.

Under pressure sunderland boss Mick McCarthy has eventually made a breakthrough in the transfer market and signed Chinese international 'Win Won Soon.'

A burglary took place at 'The Stadium of Light' last night

Charlie Hurley, sunderland legend, sporting his 5 year old 2 bob baseball boots!

when thieves broke into the main stand and entered the Trophy Room taking its entire contents. Police released a statement asking the public to be on the look out for a man with a Red Carpet.

Sunderland football club and their fans enjoyed their four seasons in the Premiership- Autumn, winter, spring, and summer!!

N.A.S.A have just announced that from now on they're sending all their trainee Astronauts to 'The Stadium of Light' to do their training, as it's the only place on earth without any atmosphere.

An unnamed sunderland player has moved house after he heard that 90% of accidents occur around the home.

Relegated and the laughing stock of English football last season, the mighty 'Black Cats,'

sunderland bounced back on their Pre-Season tour with an excellent result. Sunderland 8 Cambodia didn't!!!

Police on Wearside have arrested four men in Hendon believed to be linked to Osama Bin Laden's network. The men, who are now being questioned under 'The Terrorist Act,' have been named as Bin Thieven, Bin Muggin, Bin Dealin and Bin Twoc'in.

Nearly 90% of people working on Wearside are now banking with the Nationwide a National survey revealed today. We tried to contact one of the 362 customers, but couldn't manage to get a comment.

A new world record was set at Brands Hatch on Sunday when a bunch of Mackems changed Damon Hill's wheels in less than 5 seconds. They also removed his car stereo, spoiler, hubcaps, and wing mirrors.

Reports are coming in that there's been an outbreak of the SARS VIRUS (Severe Acute Respiratory Syndrome), in sunderland at the Stadium of Light. Apparently it's now nationwide!!

JOKES

What's the difference between secret sad Mackem Chef Lloyd Grossman and a cross-country run?
One is a pant in the country and the other is a ...!!

How many Mackem jokes are there on this page?
Only two as the rest are all true stories.

What's the difference between a Puddle and the sunderland squad?
The Puddle has more Depth.

How can you tell Billy Hardy is a Mackem?
Because he looks like one.

How many sunderland fans does it take to change a light bulb?
None! As they're quite happy living in the shadows.

A Mackem goes to Canada to be a lumberjack. The first day on the job and the boss gives him a Chainsaw & says, "Listen Mackem, I expect 100 trees felled per day, if you don't make the grade you're sacked!" Twelve hours later the Mackem staggers back into the camp and collapses. "

How many trees you done today Mackem?" asks the boss. "I managed 97 " croaks the shattered Mackem. The boss sees how pathetic he looks and gives him one last chance.
The next day after 13 hrs, the Mackem is carried in by the other loggers. "Well how many you managed today?" enquires the boss. The Mackem - half dead, just manages to speak, " 98 boss." Another logger says "Jeez boss, that Mackem might be a scummy, dirty, shitty specimen, but he's worked non-stop for 13 hrs, no lunch, tea breaks, nothing!" The boss wonders if the Mackem's Chainsaw might be faulty so he pulls the cord and the saw roars into life. The Mackem leaps up and shouts, " What's that noise!!"

LET'S ALL LAUGH AT SUNDERLAND

Thanks to the permanent football exhibition
'THE HOMES OF FOOTBALL' which is a must see
whenever you visit Ambleside in the lake district.
Who put the ball in the Mackems net... O'Brien, O'Brien

TV programmes

Home and Away
A pointless programme with Peter, Howard and now Mick roaming the country for that elusive next point.

Carry On Foxing
Sid James and the rest of the cast join sunderland FC.

Record Breakers
Roy Castle makes a comeback to host the most astounding record breakers of all time, sunderland AFC — now officially the worst team ever to play in the top flight.

Red Dwarf
Starring Milton Nunez

Film :
Going Up In The World
Kevin Phillips joins QPR.

Match Of The Day
Starring Gordon Armstrong and my arse.

Film :
The Good, The Bad and The Ugly
Featuring Malcolm MacDonald, Bernie Slaven and Eric Gates.

Knobs Landing
sunderland's first team return by plane at Teeside airport after their away match at Plymouth.

Dad's Army
Starring sunderland's first team squad.

Mission Impossible
sunderland try to get promoted

The Bill
Comedian Bob Murray wonders how on earth he'll manage to feed his stable of donkeys as he's let all his customers in for nowt.

Bargain Hunt
David Dickinson gives Mick McCarthy £200 to buy a new Sewpa Kev.

Blankety Blank
Highlights of SAFC v Seaham Red Star

Film :
Scrooge
Starring Bob Murray and introducing Mick McCarthy

The Great Escape
A gripping film starring a cast of thousands trying desperately to escape the Stadium Of Shite after yet another nightmare opening 45 minutes.

The Office
This admin. department drama looks to be coming to an end as relegated sunderland make over 80 redundancies including all their ticket office staff.

Top Of The Flops
Featuring Tore Andre Flo Band, Spandau Babb, McAteers For Fears, Kyle Minogue, Tom Peeters and Lee & The Thome Robinson Band

Crimewatch
Live every week from Pennywell.

Nationwide round-up
A series that looks as though it could run and run, despite the poor quality on offer.

Sale Of The Century
It's all got to go at the SOL.

Little Shithouse On The Prairie
Nunez goes home.

Only Fools & Horses
A very small cast now, as a tiny crowd watches Kevin Kyle and friends try to play football, starring Howard Wilkinson and Red Rum.

I'm a celebrity, get me out of here
Steve Cram tries to get out of the SOL at half-time.

Steptoe and Son
Bob Stokoe and Mick Buxton collect scrap.

Play Away
Featuring Chris Makin

Father Ted
Starring Mick McCarthy

The Weakest Link
A very slow moving programme with Mick McCarthy taking over from Anne Robinson. He's spoilt for choice as he tries to reduce his forty man squad of rubbish.

All Creatures Great And Small
Starring Alan Shearer and Milton Nunez

Grandstand
Unfortunately we have to make do with repeats as sunderland's countdown to relegation ended some time ago.

Casualty
Yet another manager bites the dust at SOL.

Stars In Their Eyes
Billy Hardy's latest comeback.

Top Cat
Everybody remembers where they were on that fateful day the mackems received their Top Cat/Dogs trophy. Again we have to repeat this original as unfortunately no further programmes were made in the following seasons due to the trophy going missing and a significant lack of interest from the local press.

MAKEM TELEVISION

And some news just in...

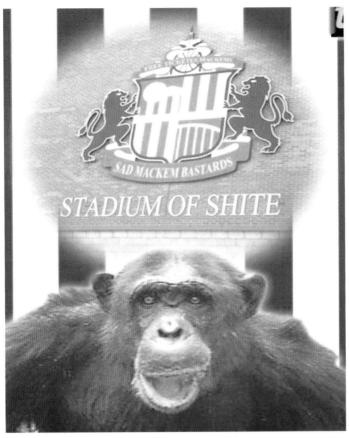

STADIUM OF SHITE

SAD MACKEM BASTARDS

Football mad Father Dean Harvey has named his newborn son after the entire playing staff of his beloved sunderland fc. 'Complete bunch of Donkeys and absolute shite' weighed in at 8lbs 6oz.

Blunderland are asking their kit manufacturers to put their 'Reg Varney' sponsors logo on the backs of their shirts and the numbers on the front so that it looks like they're attacking.

sunderland today announced that they have a new club sponsorship deal with Tampax. Their chairman said it should help them over this bad period.

There's been some great news for Bob Murray and the Directors of sunderland today, when Mick McCarthy pulled off an amazing transfer coup. The likeable Wearside boss signed legendary Dutchman Van Gogh on a free transfer!! He can't pass, shoot, dribble and doesn't get many goals but he can draw a good crowd.

JOKES

Did you hear about the sunderland fan that cleaned his ears out and his head caved In!

Why do Mackems wear Red and White Hats?
So they know which end to wipe.

Why did God make urine yellow?
So the Mackems would know if they're coming or going.

Why do cars in sunderland have small steering wheels?
So they can drive with their handcuffs on.

What do Mackems and sperm have in common?
One in 3,000,000 has a chance of becoming a human beings.

What's the difference between Michael Gray and God?
God doesn't think he is Michael Gray.

What's the difference between Tommy Sorensen and Pamela Anderson?
Pamela has only got two tits in front of her.

What's the difference between a taxi and sunderland's defence?
A Taxi only lets in four at a time.

What do you call a Mackem in a White Shell Suit?
The Bride.

What do you call a pregnant Mackem woman?
A Dope carrier.

You're trapped in a room with a Rattlesnake, a Tiger, and a Mackem.

You've got a gun with only two bullets, what do you do?
You shoot the Mackem twice just to make sure.

What's the difference between a Mackem Lad and a Mackem Lass?
The Mackem Lass has the higher Sperm count.

How do you get a Mackem out of the bath?
Put some water in it.

How do you get four sunderland fans on a stool?
Turn it upside down.

What have Michael Jackson and Tommy Sorensen got in common?
They both wear gloves for no apparent reason.

An intelligent Geordie, an intelligent Mackem, and Santa Claus are sitting in a room. There is a twenty pound note in the middle of the floor, who pick's it up?
The intelligent Geordie, as the other two don't exist.

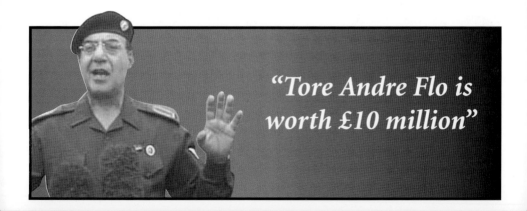

"Tore Andre Flo is worth £10 million"

sunderland su

Kevin Phillips Jigsaw
(£9.99)
(Goes to pieces in the box)

Best of sunderland FC video
(£12.99)
All the highlights and the
action, from the past 30 years.
This five-minute video is a
perfect gift for any fan.

sunderland FC official Tablecloth
(£2.99)
Suitable for all occasions, but does tend
to slip down the table after a while.

Cow Sheds & Shitholes
(£14.99)
This book lists all the grounds
where you will be visiting over the
next decade. (Apologies if you've
already visited most before.)

Black Cat Champagne
(£29.99)
Best chilled for 156 years,
ideal for your next celebration.

safc since the war 'DVD'
(£19.99)
This DVD covers the YO YO
years since the 2nd World war.

Dumb and Dumber Video Box Set
Stars Howard Wilkinson and Steve Cotterill
in the follow up to Premier Passions.

Black Cat Goalkeepers Gloves
(£8.99)
A must for fans sitting behind the
goal or near the corner flags,
just in case you do ever get a shot.

Status Quo Live C.D.
(£9.99)
Live from the Stadium of light, the
concert that opened the new stadium.
Starting with Rockin' all over the
world and ending with Down, Down.

pporters Shop

ITEMS FOR SALE

safc Gents Watch
(27.99)
As worn by Mickey Mouse

Mackem Sanitary Towels
(50p each)
The Niall Quinn Sanitary towels,
in one week, out the next.

sunderland Bra
(£9.99)
For your lass! This Bra is
available in your club
colours and has a low level
of support and no cups.

Ftm - Free Ticket Mackems
Choose from our fantastic
range of FTM gear. Not to
be worn in the Metrocentre
in case you get chinned.

Mackem Harry Houdini Kit
(£54.75)
To help you escape from the
stadium of Light in the
Half-time interval when the
club locks you in.

Red and White Condoms
(3 for £1.00)
Ideal for the pricks at
the Stadium of Light

ALS fanzine subscription
(£3.00 a season)
Subscribe to our new fanzine
'A Laughing Stock' (ALS)

JOKES

Howard Wilkinson and Kevin Phillips were sitting in a bar on the Quayside with a little dog on a stool in between them. As they were having a drink in walked a man, who walked up to the dog lifted its tail, bent down and had a good look before he silently turned round and left the bar. They looked at the barman puzzled, and then in came a second man who did exactly the same as the first. Ten minutes later a third man came in walked up to the dog lifted its tail, bent down and had a good look. Before he had a chance to leave the Barman asked, "Why did you come into my pub and without buying a beer, lift the dog's tail up?" The man replied, "There's a bloke standing outside telling everyone that there's a dog sitting on a stool with two arseholes in this pub!!"

This bloke is doing 120mph down the motorway when a Cop with a radar gun catches him and pulls him over. "What's the hurry?" asks the Cop. "I'm late for work" came the reply from the driver. "What do you do for a living" The bloke responds, "I'm a Rectum Stretcher," The Cop says "What is a Rectum Stretcher?" The bloke says yes I start with a finger then work my way up to two fingers, before I eventually get a hand in, then both hands and slowly stretch it until it's about six feet wide!" The Cop asks, "So what do you do with a six foot arsehole?" "Well, you give him a red and white striped shirt and call it a Mackem!!"

Old Geordie was on his death bed so he called in his son and handed him his Newcastle Season Ticket and croaked "Here son get rid of this and get me a season ticket for sunderland." "But Dad" says the bairn "You've been a Toon supporter all your life," "Aye, but I'd rather one of them buggers died, than one of us."

British troops have found the cave where Bin Laden was hiding during the invasion of Afghanistan, unfortunately he has fled, but they have found his diary. It reads as follows:
Monday: Just stayed in cave.
Tuesday: Stayed in cave again.
Wednesday: Never left the cave all day.
Thursday: Sick of being stuck in this cave, bored out of my head.
Friday: Stayed in cave all day, feel suicidal as can't take anymore.
Saturday: Went to watch sunderland play at the Stadium of Light. Wish I'd stayed in the fucking cave!!!

A Geordie was stuck in traffic for an hour at Swan House roundabout on his way to work one morning, when he saw a Traffic Cop coming towards his car. "What's the hold up officer?" he asked, to which came the reply, "There's a Suicidal Mackem in the middle of the road crying that he's lost his job, his wife's ran off with his brother and that his football team has been relegated." "And he's threatening to douse himself in petrol and set himself alight, so I'm having a whip round for him." Geordie asked, "So how much have you got Officer?" "Oh, just about a gallon, but people are still siphoning!!"

What do you call a Mackem at a European match?
A Turncoat.

The sunderland team are on a boat to their end of season tour. Then for some unknown reason the boat begins to sink. Who gets saved?
The whole nation.

What have sunderland and a nappy got in common?
Piss up front and crap at the back.

"One picture is worth ten thousand words"

... Frederick R. Barnard (1921).

"Sunderland a big club? ... My arse!" - Jim Royle (2002) ...Probably.

Gary Kempster, Dunston Mag

SKY SPORTS   TIF   ON SALE 4TI

THIS IS FOOTBALL 2003

| Home Page | Fixtures | Results | Tables | Video | Live Scores | Sky Live | Your View |

Football
Premier League
Nationwide League
Scottish Leagues
Euro 2004
Cup Competitions

FIXTURES

All kick-off times are in UK local time.

Tuesday October 1

Worthington Cup
Second Round

Brentford v Middlesbrough — 19:45

Cambridge Utd v Sunderland — 19:45

UEFA Champions League
Group E

Feyenoord v Dynamo Kiev — 19:45

Juventus v Newcastle — 19:45

Official Press Release sunderland F.C.

The Stadium of Shite, Queerside.

Directors:	Isaac Hunt.	Treasurer:	Ronald Biggs
	R. Soales.	Auditors:	Lowe & B. Hold
	Hugh Pratt.	Team Coach:	1976 (52 Seater)
	Mustapha Crapp.	Chief Scout:	Baden Powell
Trustees:	Netto & Poundstretcher	Manager:	Harry Houdini
Secretary:	Helen Back	Club Sponsor:	Nationwide

In recent years we have not enjoyed the best of fortunes and unfortunately start the new season in the First Division. However, all is not doom and gloom and I can assure all you sunderland supporters out there, that we as a club will be trying our utmost to win a football match this time round.

We look forward to meeting up with our old friends Walsall, Wigan, Gillingham, Preston and Rotherham who we played against in our fantastic and historic 1987-88 Third Division campaign. We also look forward to playing the mighty Crewe Alexander who's ground capacity is 10,046 and have never won an honour in English football. Luckily Gillingham's Priestfield Stadium and Walsall's Bescot Stadium are larger grounds, both holding 10,700, so we can expect to nearly fill the away section if we put a couple of coaches on and maybe a mini bus.

In the last fortnight we the Board, in response to supporters demands, have tried to bring in some new faces. Household names such as Beckham, Redknapp, Gascoigne, Savage and Campbell have been approached, but unfortunately Victoria, Louise, Jill, Lily and Naomi have all knocked us back, claiming there are enough tits in the team already.

Our Pre-Season Tour/Booze Cruise to France proved to be a hit with the players, especially the Piss heads and smokers in the squad, who responded with a fine nearly victorious performance against a 'Calais Dock Workers' eleven, who had just finished a 12 hour shift. Only 8 lucky breakaways by the Garlic eating labourers halted our plans for a clean sheet and a goalless draw, but we aren't too downbeat as we iron out all our problems in the practice matches.

Our three Chinese trialists' from the Wan King take-away have returned to their homeland. We Won Wonce, Ow Long Sinse and Foo King Yonksago were very impressive in training, but unfortunately we couldn't see them in a match situation as their shift patterns at Nissan clashed with all our efforts, apart from the 4am match v Crowtree Leisure centre under 12's, which was called off due to irate parents. Mr & Mrs Kyle and Michael Proctor's family weren't prepared to allow their son's play out, in the middle of the night.

As always we like to get you the supporter involved in any major changes at the club, so we'd like you to help by sending any suggestions you may have for Money Making schemes. We already hope to have 'Monkey Tennis' at Crowtree Leisure Centre with guest speaker Peter Reid. Also popular with the kids our Celebrity Charity Donkey rides, featuring Niall Quinn and Tore Andre Flo on Whitburn Beach in September, where young fans get a chance to meet the stars and sit on their backs.

JOKES

A White Dick wears a White condom, a Black Dick wears a Black condom, a Thin Dick wears a Thin condom, and a Thick Dick wears a sunderland shirt!!

The Mackems have sent their best woman to kill Bin Laden. Unfortunately she got her Anthrax mixed up with her Tampax and poisoned the wrong cunt!!

Nunez, the sunderland dwarf, was in Annabel's nightclub in sunderland, when he turned to a leggy brunette and said, "Can I smell your Fanny?" "Absolutely not ye little shit"

she angrily replied. Nunez continued "Well it must be your feet then!"

A young lad is on his way to The Stadium Of Light with his Dad to watch the England v Turkey Match, Euro 2004 qualifier. He asks "What time does it kick-off tonight Dad?" "About every five minutes" came his father's reply.

Why don't Mackems eat pickles?
Because they can't get their heads into the jars.

Why are Ice Hockey goal minders and Mackem girls alike?
Because they both change their pads after 3 periods.

What do you get if you cross a Zebra with a Mackem?
Nothing whatsoever, as Zebras are too intelligent to shag Mackems.

What do you call A Mackem with an I.Q. of 180?
Silksworth. . .

Why don't they have Ice Cubes in sunderland?
Because they lost the recipe.

What do you call a Mackem lass with half a brain?
Gifted!

How many Mackems does it take to pave a Driveway?
It depends on how thin you slice them.

Did you hear about Geordie Kneivel?
He tried to jump over twelve Mackems in a steamroller!

Why do Mackems not have Cheque Books?
Because it's hard to sign your name with Spray Paint.

How do you Brainwash a mackem?
Give them an Enema.

What's the difference between a Mackem girl and a Ten-pin Bowling Ball?
You can only stick three fingers in a Bowling Ball.

"sunderland will qualify for Europe in my grandchildren's lifetime"

Football Supporters Survey

Which team do you really support? The survey below has been compiled by experts and is without doubt the best way to find out, which Club you support and what kind of football fan you really are. Have you got what it takes to support Newcastle United, maybe sunderland, or even Manchester United? Answer the following questions to find out which club is closest to your heart.

My first ever match was:
a) When my Dad took me for my 4th Birthday
b) Can't remember who we played but I know we lost
c) When my parents bought me a portable TV for Christmas

I support my team because:
a) I live nearby
b) I live nearby, but wish I didn't
c) I long for European nights, Wembley finals, winning every week, lots of media coverage, and basically my local team is shite.

Watching my team:
a) Has its ups and downs
b) is like watching wet paint stay wet
c) is great on my new TV

It's costly supporting my team because:
a) The board are greedy Buggers
b) I keep betting on us at the Ladbrokes booth
c) Away shirts and third strips cost a bloody fortune these days

Since the Taylor Report on Safety at football:
a) I sit down and sing, but spend a lot of the time standing also
b) We're still playing crap and getting relegated
c) I've fixed a rope ladder to my bedroom window and bought a seatbelt for my armchair

The San Siro is:
a) a fantastic stadium, which holds some fabulous memories
b) a Mexican Hat.
c) On Channel four every Sunday

To see some action in Europe next year:
a) I'll just get my passport out
b) I've booked a Cheap family package holiday to Turkey
c) I'll be subscribing to Sky Sports and watching ITV

Phil Neville:
a) is intensely ugly
b) will never sign for us in a million years
c) is on lots of posters on my bedroom wall

The sort of player who I'd like to see playing for us:
a) would give 100% every match
b) would never sign in a million years
c) will sign if he's paid enough

Football Violence:
a) is on the decline
b) is what I feel like at quarter to five
c) is throwing your pizza box at the TV set.

Newcastle is:
a) The Greatest place on earth, ask anybody
b) Where I fly to Turkey from
c) After Manchester United on the Teletext A to Z

Manchester is:
a) A stinking slum and thank God I don't live there
b) A stinking slum, but it's Beverly Hills compared to our town
c) About 5 hours away by coach

sunderland is:
a) A shithole, which we won't have to visit for a very long time

b) Twinned with Beirut

c) Never on the television

Alan Shearer is:
a) The Greatest striker alive, if not ever
b) A twat, I hate him
c) Always on my television as an expert or scoring for those Northerners

A penalty is usually given:
a) all too frequently against us
b) for a handball or a foul
c) when one of our players falls over near the box

Your team wins the title. Do you:
a) Celebrate for a month or two then look forward to next season
b) Wake up. Of course it was all a dream.
c) Eat a KFC Family size Chicken Bucket, then stroll down Exeter high street.

When I die:
a) my ashes will be scattered over our pitch
b) we still won't have won anything
c) nobody will care

HOW DID YOU SCORE?

Mainly A's -
You support Newcastle United

Mainly B's -
You support sunderland, and you deserve it!

Mainly C's -
We don't want to know, You total Penis!

We cannot match Toon

By JEREMY ROBINSON

UNDER-FIRE Sunderland chairman Bob Murray has begged fans not to compare the club to their North East rivals . . . and admitted the Black Cats are currently the region's poor relations.

As the beleaguered Wearsiders battle for their Premiership lives, Murray said the club's situation is completely different to Newcastle and Middlesbrough.

"Our prices are half Newcastle's prices – you just can't compare the clubs, they're not to compare," he said.

MURRAY

"We're stuck between a massive city that's vibrant like Newcastle – and Middlesbrough with a benefactor who puts £20 million-a-year into the club.

(Sunday Sun) - 'They charge half Newcastle's prices and can't compare with a massive vibrant city like the Toon. A bit of a change from always having one more (empty) seat.'

JOKES

Once upon a time in the Kingdom of Heaven, God went missing for six days. Eventually, Michael the Archangel found him on the seventh day resting. He inquired of God, "Where have you been?" God sighed a deep sigh of satisfaction and proudly pointed downwards through the clouds, "Look Michael, look what I've made." said God.

Archangel Michael looked puzzled and said, "What is it?" "It's a planet," replied God, "and I've put LIFE on it. I'm going to call it Earth and it's going to be a great place of balance."

"Balance?" inquired Michael, still confused. God explained, pointing to different parts of Earth, "For example, North America will be a place of great opportunity and wealth while South America is going to be poor; the Middle East over there will be a hotspot and Russia will be a cold spot. Over there I've placed a continent of white people and over there is a continent of black people," God continued, pointing to different countries. "This one will be extremely hot and humid while this one will be very cold and covered in ice." The Archangel, impressed by God's work, then pointed to a small area of land and said, "What's that?" "Ah," said God. "That's Newcastle, the most glorious place on Earth. There are beautiful people; a great football team, an impressive cathedral, and home to a number of the world's greatest ever pop groups. The people from Newcastle are going to be modest, intelligent and humorous and they're going to be found travelling the world. They'll be extremely sociable, hard-working and high-achieving, and they will be known throughout the world as diplomats and carriers of peace." Michael gasped in wonder and admiration but then proclaimed, "What about balance, God? You said there will be BALANCE!" God replied wisely, "Wait until you see the wankers I'm putting next to them in sunderland."

What's the difference between a Mackem and a supermarket trolley?
A Supermarket trolley has a mind of it's own.

What happens when a Mackem takes Viagra?
He gets a bit taller.

An anxious woman goes to her Doctor. "Doctor," she asks nervously, "can I get pregnant from anal intercourse?" "Certainly," replies the doctor, "Where do you think Mackems come from?"

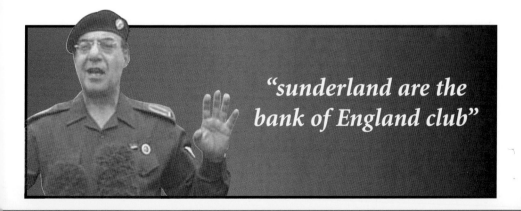

"sunderland are the bank of England club"

An Ode to Bob Murray

(musical background supplied by Eminem)

Dear Murray, I wrote but you still ain't callin
I left my mobile, my home phone and e-mail at the bottom
I sent 2 letters before transfer deadline; you must not a got 'em
It probably was a problem at the post office or somethin'
Maybe you didn't even look at 'em just left them and forgot 'em?
But anyways, fuck it, what's been up man, I'm glad I caught ya?
My girlfriend wants a word too, I'm bout to be a father
If we don't start winning soon, I'm starting to wish I'd worn a johnny
It's pissing my Mother in Law off too, say sorry
I had a friend kill himself over some club who didn't respect him.
I know you probably hear this everyday, don't ignore us we're not dim.
Don't go underground and make us believe it's just a scam
Tell us what's happening, we are sick and tired of this man
You gonna cause a Ruckus too like we all saw on Sat
Anyways, I hope you get this man, hit me back, just to chat
Truly yours, disgruntled fan, this is Dan.

CHORUS

The Nationwide's calling I'm wondering why
I get outta bed at all
Saturday morning rain clouds up my window
It's almost time for football
And why are we being led by Mickey Gray,
I've got Reyna on my wall
It reminds me, when did it all go bad,
All go bad..

VERSE 2

Dear Bobby, you still ain't called or wrote, when you get the chance
I'm getting mad, I think it's fucked up you don't answer fans.
If you didn't want to talk to me outside the Stadium You didn't have to
I didn't want an autograph I came to whack you
And my little brother, man. He's only 6 years old.
We waited in the blistering cold for you for 4 hours and ya just said no.
That's pretty shitty man, I ended up in Idols
Drunk 10 pints of Stella, walked into a tree, bruised my balls.
I ain't that mad, but I just don't like bein' lied to.
Remember back in September, things would be better, said you
We signed Flo and Stewart, how much did you pay???
Oh and there was Matty Piper You said put him on the wing and he would beat ya
Can you understand or acknowledge that you were wrong?

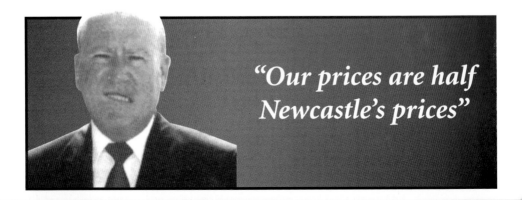

"Our prices are half Newcastle's prices"

Sacking Reidy, okay, but fucking Howard Wilkinson? Shit Murray, couldn't you tell we were already depressed And do the team realise the honour of the badge on their chest?
Sometimes they can't be arsed do you know that makes us bleed
Do they wear Maybelline, wear dresses and sip tea?
See, everything you say is fake, and you lost our respect cause you
Bullshit
My girl's leaving me, I'm depressed and it's your fault you git
But nobody knows exactly what you think, no one does
What's the story, what is happening, what's up?
You've gotta call me man. It's the fans that will lose.
Sincerely yours, Dan. P.S: Sell Babb he is poo.

CHORUS

VERSE 3

Dear Mr. "I'm too good to call or write the fans"
The next letter I send will explode on your ass
It's been 18 months, 8 wins. We don't deserve it?
No improvement, no hope, we don't expect it to be perfect
We don't complain and boo, I know you hear it People are home early now cos what we witness on match day is admit it,
total shit
Hey Bob, think of the millions you miss next year because of Sky Live
You know the song at the beginning of the match "Dance of the Knights"

Well the build up, the drama, what a joke, can't you see we're drowning?
Sort it out, sack the board, have you ever gone out on a limb
So that's how it is, you could've rescued us from downing
Now it's too late, it's the Nationwide and our derby is against Burnley
And all I wanted was a lousy letter or a call.
I hope you know you ripped us off, I prefer watching Millwall.
We love the club; we could of worked together, think about it
You ruined it now, you appointed Wilko, and quite frankly he has lost it
We are propping up the table not leading it, can't you see?
See Bob, if you had just come to us to talk.
We could've told you he's pap; we would've preferred Kelly Brook
But we believed in you, we gave you time, but admit it.
It's a decision
that you rue
Cause when we go down, who will suffer more, me or is it you?
Well gotta go I' just crossing the Wear Bridge now
See you soon, I've got a gun, we are going to work this shit out?

CHORUS

VERSE 4

Dear Bob, I meant to write you sooner, but I've just been busy.
I've been talking to Howard, he isn't mental, or is he?

Look I really must say it's not my fault, decisions were made wrong,
For this and for that
I had to line my pockets and have a quick nap.
I'm sorry if you feel what we have done is just poo
Don't think I did that shit intentionally, just to piss you.
And anyway, it's the fans fault you shouldn't boo
I say that shit just clownin' dawg, c'mon, how fucked up is you?
You bring up good issues Bob, but I can't comment, ask my mum
I talk shit, can't you see it's pouring out my bum
I'm off on holiday, for some sun, can't stand this bad weather.
I fear the worse, I'm off with my rent boy lover
Ha, don't think I care, I'm loaded, hear it every day pull the other
What you going to do eh? Could you do any better? Do you think I read your letters?
Is looking after your own such a crime?
You made me sack Reidy, the scouse twat was doing just fine
Did the Wilko appointment not inspire you Bob?
He is only a little mad, try to understand that I'm not a real fan.
You won't do any crazy shit You're all talk, you make me sick.
You want the club, go on make a bid
I sold my shares at 3 quid! Enough of this bullshit, someone is at my door, adios, toodle-oo
Shit, an angry mob, and it's, oh it's you. DAMN!

At the height of *Friday Night Live*'s success I decided to do Loads' Northern equivalent. The eighties boom seemed very much a Southern phenomenon. Touring round the country doing gigs, I was aware of the North–South divide – the South full of yuppies and new housing, the North full of derelict industries and closed-down mines. I'd spent a lot of time in Newcastle, doing gigs and spots on Channel Four's *The Tube*. I loved the Geordie people, their pride in their city and their sense of humour. I'd also hung around with the boys who wrote *Viz* comic, which was then just taking off. I really wanted to do a character for the North to counteract Loads the Southerner. So Paul, Charlie, Geoff Perkins, Chris and I cobbled a sketch together. The accent was the next big thing – the Geordie accent is not the easiest to learn for a 'Southern puff' like me. So I had to send Chris Donald, the editor of *Viz*, a copy of the script in Newcastle. He then rang up my answering machine and read it out phonetically on to the tape, which I played to myself again and again until I'd got the voice as best I could.

He worked fine on the programme, and the Geordies I met in the street were very nice about him – but said my accent was crap! They said I sounded 'like a bloody Mak'em'. I'd never heard the word 'Mak'em' and it turned out to mean someone from Sunderland – Geordies like to think that their neighbours are thickheads, good only for ordering about: 'Yer mak'em dee this and mak'em dee that.'

The word was to come in handy when I faced my biggest Buggerallmoney challenge – doing a gig in Newcastle where I had to face two thousand pissed-up Geordies on their home turf. Buggerallmoney came on to huge applause, but as soon as I've gone, 'I've got buggerallmoney and I'm a Geordie me!' I had howls of abuse from the back of the hall: 'You're not a Geordie, yer big Southern puff.' Immediately I hit back: 'How mon! Yer say Ah'm norra Geordie. Worrad yees know aboot that? Yer dorty greet Mak'em!!' Just knowing the word 'Mak'em' saved my bacon – I got a huge laugh and the hecklers left me in peace. I zoomed through my set as fast as I could, hoping that the quicker the words came out, the better they would sound, but at the end of the evening I asked the audience how my accent had been and two thousand people yelled in unison: 'SHITE !!'

> I asked the audience how my accent had been and two thousand people yelled in unison: 'SHITE!!'

Buggerallmoney

Taken from the excellent book 'Harry Enfield and His Humorous Chums'

EUROPEAN WAY

CLOSED

DUE TO ESSENTIAL CONSTRUCTION WORK

Welcome to sunderland!

I'll just finish this then I'll do Peter Reids face

For Sale:

Economical, reliable little runner. Two previous owners. Needs some work done. Relegation forces sale. Any offers accepted. Trade-in welcome.

Bobby **Kerr**

Hands up all the clowns
Who used to play for
Sunderland**!**

"He's a **tramp,** he's **small,** he **looks**
like **B**obby **B**all **Bobby Kerr**, **Bobby Kerr"**

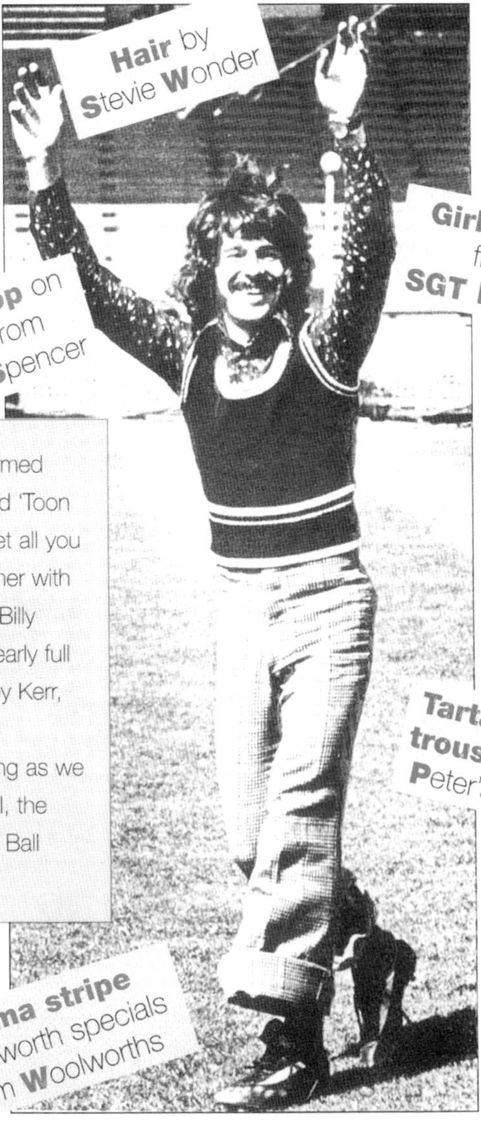

Hair by
Stevie **W**onder

Bobby the **clown ~~prince~~**
of football

Girls shirt
from
SGT Peppers

Tank top on
loan from
Frank **S**pencer

We have recently been informed
that Sunderland fans actually read 'Toon
Army News'! So not wanting to let all you
mackems down we've got together with
top fashion retailers Oxfam and Billy
Smarts Circus to produce this nearly full
colour poster of your hero, Bobby Kerr,
or is it Billy Hughes ? We're not
bothered what he is called as long as we
all agree he looks like Bobby Ball, the
only difference being that Bobby Ball
is well known.

Tartan check
trousers from
Peter's **S**tores

Puma stripe
Woolworth specials
from **W**oolworths

JOKES

A little kid gets on a bus and sits right behind the driver, who is driving the bus wearing a sunderland scarf. He starts yelling, "If my dad was a bull and my Mam was a cow I'd be a little bull." The Mackem starts getting mad at the noisy kid, who continues with, "If my Dad was an elephant and my Mam a girl elephant I would be a little elephant." The kid goes on with several animals until the Mackem gets angry and yells at the kid, "What if your Dad was gay and your Mam was a Prostitute?!" The kid smiles and says, "Then I would be a Mackem!"

Q: How does a Mackem change a light bulb?
A: He asks the prison guard.

Q: What's the difference between a Mackem Lass and a Kit Kat.
A: You can only get 4 fingers in a Kit Kat.

Q: How did the Mackem find his sister in the woods?
A: Just Fine!!

Howard Wilkinson walks into a Sperm Donor Bank, "I'd like to donate some sperm" he says to the receptionist. "Certainly Sir" replies the receptionist, "have you donated before?". "Yes," replies Wilko "you should have my details on your computer."
"Oh yes, I've found your details" says the receptionist "but I see you're going to need help. Shall I call your wife for you?"
"Why do I need help?" asks Wilko. The receptionist replies "Well, it says on your record that you're a useless Wanker..."

Three football fans, all in their nineties, are sitting in church when God appears and grants them one question each.
The Geordie asks, "When will the Toon win the European Champions League?" God replies, "Not this season but next." Geordie says, "I'll be dead by then!"
The smoggy asks, "When will Boro ever play in Europe?"
God replies, "Within the next 10 years"
The smoggy croaks, "But I'll be dead by then"
The Mackem asks, "When will sunderland win the Premiership?"
God replies, "I'll be dead by then ye Knacker!!"

Mick McCarthy bursts into the changing room at the Stadium of Light and announces, "Because we have been relegated without a win since Christmas, I'm going to bring in some new faces in the summer." Stephen Wright shouts out, "Can I have one please boss?"

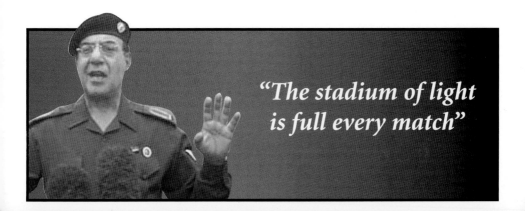

"The stadium of light is full every match"

SUNDERLAND CARING CLUB

Dear season ticket holder,

The rush will soon be on for season tickets for the 2003-04 season and because in the past you have shown yourself to be a loyal supporter of this very proud club, you will be pleased to know that you can reserve yours at a special rate.

We are writing to all season ticket holders over the next few days and to give you some idea of the size of the operation, I can tell you in advance that the postage stamps alone will cost £32.56.

Over the summer the club will be making a lot of changes so that we are ready for the exciting new season ahead. Some of the deadwood amongst our playing staff will be transfer listed, so expect to say farewell to Sewpa Kev, Claire Reyna and Tommy Sorensen, as we look to bring in unknown free transfers to challenge with the likes of Wigan, Crewe, Burnley, Walsall and Gillingham.

The likes of Nicholas Medina Cake and Tore Andre Flora are our bread and butter players, who along with the likes of Steven Schwarz, Phil Babb, Jason McAteer and Eric Gates are the future of this club.

The comfort of our supporters such as yourself, is to be given top priority and one season ticket will entitle you to four seats together so that you can watch the matches lying down, or catch up on your sleep if you wish. When applying please note we are only opening the Main West Stand this season, as the Fosters Stand is to be turned into the City's first Cinema, a state of the art Popcorn Picture House. Meanwhile the Home End (North Stand) is to be turned into 'Charlie the Clown's Wacky Warehouse,' to carry on the current theme keeping those fans happy. The Metro FM Stand will be renamed the 'FTM' Stand, which will house all of the FREE TICKET MACKEMS, i.e. School kids and students.

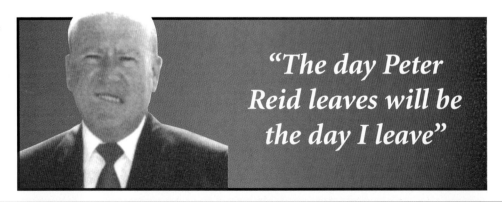

"The day Peter Reid leaves will be the day I leave"

THE STADIUM OF SHITE, WEARSIDE

Additionally, to stop any more pitch invasions we are converting the gravel around the pitch into a moat, and for a small extra charge you can sail around the pitch in a red and white Gondola and watch the match from various angles.

Finally we can offer the SUPER EXECUTIVE PACKAGE in our own luxury suites at the top of the stand. The suites are designed to supporters requests and are facing away from the pitch, giving you peace and quiet and a chance to get away from it all.

We look forward to seeing you next season and together with the help of Mick McCarthy know that we will get out of the First Division even if it means dropping down to the Second.

SEASON TICKET PRICES
(includes all League, Autoglass and Charity Matches)

	Adults	Kids
Main Stand (4 seat settee offer)	£53.67	free
Executive Suite (facing pitch)	£61.50	free
Executive Suite (facing other way)	£200.00	free
Gondolas with singing oarsman	£47.20	free
Harry Potter -3.10pm (Screen 1)	£175.00	£100.00
Wacky Warehouse season ticket	£120.00	£120.00

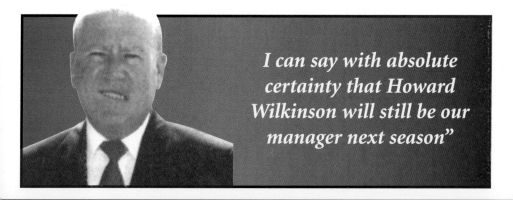

I can say with absolute certainty that Howard Wilkinson will still be our manager next season"

'Now That's What I Call Relegation'

vol. 18

MACKEM CD

Status Quo – Down Down

Cher – Gypsies, tramps & thieves

The Smiths – Heaven knows I'm miserable now

Stone Roses – Going down

Madness – Embarrassment

Vera Lynn – We'll meet again (only in the cup)

The Smiths – I know it's over

The Animals – We've gotta get outta this place

Rainbow – I surrender

Simply Red – Money's too tight to mention

Judy Collins – Send in the clowns

Fiddler's Dram – The day we went to Bangor

Carter The Unstoppable Sex Machine – Rubbish

Don McClean - Crying

AVAILABLE YET AGAIN

"We're stuck between a massive city that's vibrant like Newcastle - and Middlesbrough with a benefactor who puts £20 million a year into the club"

JOKES

A Mackem dies and goes to heaven wearing his red and white top. When he gets to the Pearly gates St Peter takes one look at him and says "Sorry no Mackems allowed in heaven," but the Mackem pleads that he is a good bloke who has led a saintly life. He says just last week I gave £15 to Help the Aged, the week before £20 to Children in need and last month another £15 to comic relief." St Peter says he will go and have a word with God. On his return he smiles at the Mackem as he says, "Here's your 50 quid back now fuck off.

Q: What is the difference between a Pit Bull and a Mackem Lass?
A: The lipstick.

Q: How do you know when a Mackem has burgled your house?
A: The Dog is pregnant and you've got no Cheese in your fridge or Chips in your freezer.

Q: When do you know when a Mackem lass has an orgasm?

A: She drops her Cheesy Chips.

Q: What's the difference between a Coach load of Mackems travelling to an away match and a hedgehog?
A: A hedgehog has all the pricks on the outside.

A Taxi Driver picks up a Mackem in the centre of sunderland and asks where he wants to go. "Tak us to the High level bridge in Newcassel marra." On the way the driver asks, "If ya divvent mind us askin like, why da ya wanna go there for?" "Whey" replies the Mackem "There's nee jobs, sunderland town is a shithole and my team has just been relegated, so there's nee point livin, I'm gonna chuck mesel ower." "Whey why don't you save some money son, I'll tak ya ta the Alexandra Bridge on the Wear?" says the cabbie taking pity on him, to which the Mackem replied. "Have ya seen the bloody queue man marra!!"

What's the difference between Marks and Spencer and Tore Andre Flo?
With Marks and Spencer you always get a full refund for unwanted purchases.

This little piggy went to market

This little piggy stayed at home

This little piggy had a bad day

ODE TO sunderland

(Sung to the theme of The Blaydon races)

T'was on April the 25th in 1993
That 30,000 and the rest did go along to see
The Mackems and their crappy team get egg upon their faces
But strangely though the Leazes End was full of empty spaces

CHORUS
Oh me lads the Mackems got a hiding
And down into Division 2 is where the twats are sliding
It's great to see the Roker shits dropping down a few more places
While all the Geordies take the piss and sing the Blaydon Races

The rain fell down the night before like Britain's own monsoon
The ref said "aye we play the game, me money's on the Toon"
The match kicked off amid the rain, the Toon were soon attacking
It poured and poured, cos Christ the Lord was peeing on the mackems

CHORUS

The mackems went to pieces, as the Toon fans were so loud
So Butcher tried to alter that by kicking into the crowd
His side were crap his midfield didn't know where they were going
And how the Leazes went berserk when Armstrong won a throw in

CHORUS

Poor butcher went from bad to worse and fouled outside the area
The mackems tried to form a wall cos things were getting scarier
Then Norman froze upon his line as if he'd seen a ghost
As Sellars scored the winning goal assisted by the post

CHORUS

To celebrate the victory the pubs all had a lock-in
The mackems just went back to work a burgling and a twocking
If they're not in the Conference before the decade's over
We'll go and get a blowjob off that dog Navratilova

CHORUS

JOKES

There was a Mackem, a Geordie and Claudia Scheiffer sitting together in a carriage in a train going down to London. Suddenly the train went through a tunnel and as it was an old style train, there were no lights in the carriages and it went completely dark. Then there was a kissing noise and the sound of a really loud slap. When the train came out of the tunnel, Claudia Schiffer and the Geordie were sitting as if nothing had happened and the Mackem had his hand against his face as if he had been slapped there. The Mackem was thinking: 'The Geordie fella must have kissed Claudia Schiffer and she missed him and slapped me instead.' Claudia Schiffer was thinking: 'The Mackem fella must have tried to kiss me and actually kissed the Geordie and got slapped for it.' And the Geordie was thinking: 'this is great. The next time the train goes through a tunnel I'll make another kissing noise and slap that Mackem bastard again.'

A Mackem fan walks into a pub with his dog just as the football scores come on the TV. The announcer says that sunderland have lost 3-0 and the dog immediately rolls over on its back, sticks its paws up in the air and plays dead. "That's amazing," says the barman. "What does it do when they win?" The Mackem Fan scratches his head for a couple of seconds and finally replies: " I Don't know.... I've only had the dog for five months.

There once was a Mackem man who was so proud of the fact that he had six kids that he insisted on calling his wife 'Mother of Six.' His wife hated this name and asked him repeatedly not to call her that. But he was a stubborn Mackem and was very proud that he had six kids.

One evening they were at a dinner party given by his company, and it was getting close to the time that they should be leaving. The husband yelled to his wife from across the room, "Mother of Six, are you ready to go?"

Annoyed with his question, she yelled back, "In a minute, Father of Two!"

A Mackem visits an Orchard and asks how much the apples are. "Pick as many as you like for a Fiver" came the reply. "Oh well in that case give me a Tenner's worth," shouted the Mackem.

Mick McCarthy is in his office when he looks out his window and see's a young teenage ginger lad playing football in the club car park. He watches in amazement as the lad shows off his excellent ball skills. The lad is so good that McCarthy opens the window and shouts down to him, "Here son would you like to come and play for sunderland?" The lad looks up and replies, "No thanks I get enough stick off my pals about the colour of my hair."

"The manager has told us to make sure we have a smile on our faces for everyone we come across over the next two months or so"

A Mackem woman and a Mackem baby come into the doctor's surgery. She was told to go into a room and wait for the doctor. After arriving there, the doctor examined the Mackem baby and asked the woman, "Is he breast fed or on the bottle?" "Breast fed," she replied. "Well, strip down to your waist," the doctor ordered. She did. He pressed, kneaded and pinched both breasts for a while in a detailed examination. Motioning to her to get dressed he said, "No wonder this baby is hungry. You don't have any milk." "Naturally," she said, "I'm his Grandma. But I'm really glad I came."

Kevin Phillips leaves sunderland and signs for Tottenham Hotspur for a fee of 2 million pounds. Just before his league debut the manager Glenn Hoddle pulls him to one side and says, "As it's your first game Kev, I'm going to pull you off at half-time." To which Phillips replied, "Bloody hell, we only used to get an Orange at sunderland!!"

A sunderland fan rings his Geordie workmate up and says "Come around here and help me with this Jigsaw puzzle, I don't even know where to start as all the pieces look the same." The Geordie say's "Well what's it supposed to be?" "Well according to the picture on the front of the box, it's supposed to be a great big giant Chicken." Geordie decides to go over and help

the Mackem. When he enters the house the Mackem is sitting scratching his head and has got the pieces all over the table spread out. The Geordie goes over picks up the box and whacks the Mackem straight over the head with the box, shouting "You thick twat, put the Corn Flakes back in the Box!!"

A sunderland lass was involved in a crash, and was lying flat on the roadside. The Paramedics arrived and started to attend to her.
Medic: Ok I'm going to check if you're concussed.
Lass: Ok
Medic: Ok, how many fingers have I got up?
Lass: Oh my God, I can't feel nothing, I'm paralysed from the waist down."

Did you hear about the Mackem who bought a jar of 'Chicken Tonight' from Asda, he forgot to eat it for his Supper, so he threw it out the next morning.

Tommy Sorensen has started as a Taxi Driver, he only lets four in at the weekend.

What's the difference between a Chocolate fireguard and sunderland fc? One is completely useless and the other is a Chocolate fireguard.

Why did the Mackem cross the road? Because he was stuck to the bottom of Geordie's boot.

Two Cannibals were chatting over lunch. One said, "You know I can't stand Mackems." "Forget about him," the other replied "Just eat the peas."

Did you hear about the Mackem on the generation game? He won a conveyor belt and two sliding doors.

Did you hear about the Mackem who tried to swim across the River Wear? He got tired halfway so decided to turn round and swim back.

How can you tell when a Mackem is talking shite? His lips move.

Did you hear about the Mackem lass who tried cock sucking for the first time? She choked on the feathers.

What's the difference between Ward 38 of the General Hospital and The Stadium of Light? It's less embarrassing coming out of Ward 38.

What do you call 200 Mackems at the bottom of the sea? A good start. . .

How far is sunderland from Newcastle Upon Tyne? About half an hour in a tank.

When god was giving out heads, Howard Wilkinson thought he'd said sheds so he ordered a wooden one.

How long does it take a Wearside girl to have a shit? About nine months.

What's the best thing ever to come out of sunderland? An empty Bomber plane.

The most popular car sticker in sunderland? "A Dog is for life not just a honeymoon."

'If you're proud to be a Geordie clap your hands' 'If you're proud to be a Mackem you must have a good sense of humour!!'

What's Red & White and makes you laugh? A bus full of sunderland fans travelling to Crewe Alexander for a league match.

A Mackem girl walks into her local Dry Cleaners and places a Dress on the counter. "I will be back tomorrow afternoon to pick it up," she announces. "Come again?" says the girl behind the desk, cupping her ear. "No" she replies, "This time it's mayonnaise."

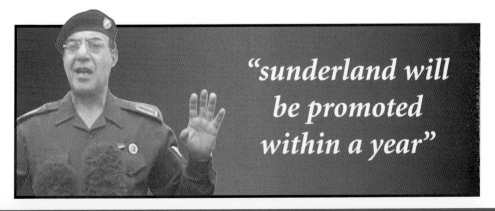

"sunderland will be promoted within a year"

IT'S A FACT

Newcastle United have never lost a match at 'The stadium of Light' in their history.

sunderland were relegated from the premeirship in the 2002/03 season with the lowest ever amount of points.

In the 1994/95 season Newcastle United's average league attendance was 34,690, while sunderland's was only 15,344!! An average difference of 19,346 less per match, the Mackems had nearly 20,000 less than their so called Geordie rivals.

sunderland sells tickets to away fans for seat numbers that don't even exist.

The Stadium of Light is a name pinched from Benfica's ground in Portugal. The ground is very similar to Derby's, Leicester's, Bolton's and Middlesbrough's.

The Mackems were originally known as 'The sunderland and District Teachers Association FC,' but changed their name due to financial difficulties! Ring any bells?

Blunderland have used 7 different home grounds over the Years including one called Newcastle Road!!

Little Watford beat the Mackems 8-0 in 1982.

In 1976 sunderland lost 9 league matches on the trot.

Walsall completed a league double over sunderland in the 88/89 Season without conceding a goal. Walsall beat sunderland 2-0 at home in front of 6,150 then completed the double winning with ease 3-0 at Roker Park in front of 14,203 clowns. The win on Wearside was the first win for Walsall in months, as they'd failed to win any of their previous 18 matches, losing their previous game 7-0 at home to Chelsea.

The same season only 8,001 turned up for sunderland's home match with Plymouth while only 1,666 turned up when they played Charlton Athletic in the Simod Cup in London.

sunderland have never beaten Newcastle United at 'The Stadium of Light' ever.

Newcastle United have not been beaten in the last 5 Tyne Wear Derbies.

The Physiotherapist at sunderland in the late eighties was called Mr S. Smelt.

In 1988 sunderland scraped together £100,000 and bought Billy Whitehurst from Reading. These were the words of Club Statistician Billy Simmons!!

Wonder why they're in trouble? (Clue - check the price)

In their last ever season at Roker Park, sunderland only filled the ground twice. They were in the Premier League yet couldn't fill the small 22,400 capacity??

The decade the 1980's got off to a terrible start for safc when NEWCASTLE UNITED hammered them 3-1 on the very first day-Jan 1st 1980.

When Newcastle United won the First Division title in 1993, sunderland missed out on relegation to the third flight of English football by only one point.

In the 1987-88 season, sunderland hung onto a 2-2 draw with 10 man Wigan in front of a third division crowd of 6,949.

Even though they finished 6th in the Second Division in 1989-90, then lost the play off final, sunderland were still promoted by default when Swindon Town were found guilty of breaking FA rules.

The Tyne & Wear Metro took over 20 years to eventually reach the village of sunderland, and guess what surprise, surprise nobody still bothers going there from Tyneside.

safc hold the record for the amount of consecutive league defeats in a row in the history of English football.

sunderland is supposed to be a city yet doesn't have a Cathedral??

99% of football fans and media watching the England v Turkey match at the stadium of light didn't stay in sunderland as there's only one hotel, a travel tavern or something.

sunderland's official website still claims that the stadium of light capacity will be extended to 58,000 even though they can't fill it now with free ticket students and school kids.

sunderland paid £8 million pounds for 30-year-old Norwegian Tore Andre Flo!!!
Honest they did, Peter Reid bought him from Rangers for £8 million.

In 1985 sunderland went 14 league matches without a win.

The stadium of light serves its fans Newcastle beers.

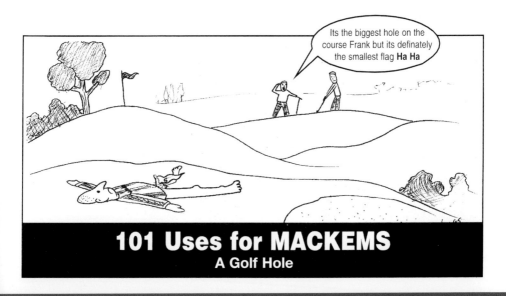

101 Uses for MACKEMS
A Golf Hole

Phil Babb, Kevin Kilbane and Jason McAteer would never in a month of Sundays, (even under Graham Taylor) get an England call up!!

sunderland are renowned for all their Irish international players yet unfortunately Phil Babb (Lambeth), Kevin Kilbane (Preston) and Jason McAteer (Birkenhead) are all actually English, not Irish??

Super goalscoring machine Kevin Phillips has been relegated with two different clubs, Watford and now sunderland.

The Stadium of Light (Not the one in Portugal - home of the famous Benfica, but the cheap not so famous one on Wearside) is the 7th different ground that the Mackems have used since they were (De) formed in 1879! Before they moved to Roker Park (6th Ground) they played at a ground called Newcastle Road!!

Kevin Phillips is not a goal-scoring machine! He only scored 11 goals in the 01/02 season and totally forgot where the onion bag was in the 02/03 Season.

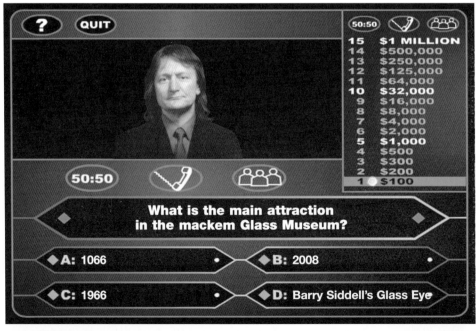

15 $1 MILLION
14 $500,000
13 $250,000
12 $125,000
11 $64,000
10 $32,000
9   $16,000
8   $8,000
7   $4,000
6   $2,000
5   $1,000
4   $500
3   $300
2   $200
1   $100

What is the main attraction in the mackem Glass Museum?

A: 1066
B: 2008
C: 1966
D: Barry Siddell's Glass Eye

Reg Vardy, who sponsor safc, is a business which sells motor vehicles and is not a comedy character from the 1970's sit-com 'On the Buses.'

On 27th January 1951, sunderland had to borrow a set of Newcastle United's Black and White striped shirts for their 4th Round FA Cup tie with Southampton. They went on to win the match 2-0 with a brace of goals from Dickie Davis (Couldn't be could it?). The same season Newcastle United won the FA Cup wearing their Black and White shirts and have never had to borrow any red and white shite shirts in their history and have never worn red and white stripes ever as Newcastle United!!

In the 1987-88 season sunderland played in the Third division. (So fucking funny)
They played clubs such as Chester City who now play in the Conference. Also that season, they played the mighty Aldershot who went into oblivion before re-inventing themselves and playing in South West Counties Division 12. Also the mighty Doncaster Rovers, the pride of Yorkshire, but now a non- league club were league opposition for mighty sunderland. That same season Newcastle United finished 8th in the top flight.

Trampwatch

Found this in the Autumn/Winter timetable of GNER services.
Vicky Cowan

At-Station Facilities

Station	Car Parking	First Class Lounge	Standard Lounge	Minimum connect time
Alnmouth	Yes	-	-	-
Arbroath	Yes	-	-	-
Aberdeen	Yes	-	-	-
Aviemore	Yes			
Berwick	Yes	Yes	Yes	-
Bradford Forster Sq.	Yes	-	-	-
Bradford Interchang	Yes	-	-	-
Darlington	Yes	Yes	Yes	7 minutes
Doncaster	Yes	Yes	Yes	7 minutes
Dunbar	Yes	-	-	-
Dundee	Yes	-	-	-
Durham	Yes	-	-	-
Edinburgh	Yes	Yes	-	10 minutes
Glasgow Central	Yes	-	-	-
Glasgow Queen St.	Yes	-	-	-
Grantham	Yes	-	-	-
Grimsby	Yes	-	-	-
Harrogate	Yes	-	-	-
Huddersfield	Yes	-	-	-
Hull	Yes	-	-	-
Inverkeithing	Yes	-	-	-
Inverness	Yes	-	-	-
Keighley	Yes			
Kirkcaldy	Yes	-	-	-
Leeds	Yes	Yes	-	10 minutes
Leuchars	Yes	-	-	-
Lincoln	Yes	-	-	-
London Kings Cross	Yes	Yes	Yes	-
Middlesbrough	Yes	-	-	-
Montrose	Yes	-	-	-
Motherwell	Yes	-	-	-
Newark	Yes	-	-	7 minutes
Newcastle	Yes	Yes	Yes	8 minutes
Northallerton	Yes	-	-	-
Perth	Yes	-	-	-
Peterborough	Yes	-	-	8 minutes
Pitlochry	Yes			
Retford	Yes	-	-	10 minutes
Scarborough	Yes	-	-	-
Selby	Yes			
Shipley	Yes	-	-	-
Skipton	Yes	-	-	-
Stevenage	Yes	-	-	-
Stirling	Yes	-	-	-
Sunderland	-	-	-	-
Wakefield	Yes	Yes	-	7 minutes
York	Yes	-	Yes	8 minutes

Sunderland F.C. Press Release

We are offering all our Season Ticket holders for the 2003/04 season the opportunity to have a say in the club's future. Unfortunately due to sacking most of the staff this summer and the closure of most of the ground, we haven't got the space or manpower to hold a Fans Forum, so instead we suggest that you split up into a Dozen groups of Five and meet at a local pub and discuss the following issues;

1. **As a leap year approaches it's time once again to change our club nickname. Our last choice 3 years ago of 'The Black Cats' hasn't been that lucky so with that in mind here's some new suggestions;**
   a) The Broken Mirrors
   b) Hoop Weep Mackems
   c) The Rokershites
   d) The Cock Hockle Tearsiders
   e) sunderland0
   f) SMB

2. **As you're well aware 'The Stadium of Light' is a name we pinched from Benfica in Portugal, so we would like to offer you the chance of renaming our ground with something more fitting;**
   a) The Riverside
   b) The Reebok Stadium
   c) Pride Park
   d) Colditz
   e) The Stadium of Plight
   f) Monkwearmouth Pit

3. **At Half-time in our home matches we would like to wake you all up by giving you some entertainment. What would you like at Half time?**
   a) The Seaburn Casuals fighting Lions in a cage
   b) The Boldon Colliery Brass Band on ecstasy Morris Dancing
   c) Throwing fruit and car wing mirrors at Eric Gates and Lawrie McMenemy
   d) The Pennywell Teenage Mums Pram Race.
   e) To be let out of the ground and a taxi home.

4. **As from the new season we will be doing our own catering, so please put a tick next to the type of food you would like to see inside the stadium.**
   a) Chips
   b) Chips and Cheese
   c) Cheesy Chips
   d) Cheesy Chips with Chips
   e) Cheesy Chips in a bun
   f) Cheesy chip pies
   g) Cheesy chip pasties
   h) Bovril

5. **We plan to use the Stadium every day of the week not just on Saturdays for our Nationwide matches, especially now that we won't have to play on Sundays and Mondays. Below is a list of ideas we have for all the family.**
   a) Basket Weaving with Kevin Kilbane
   b) Irish Dancing with McCarthy and 73% of the first team
   c) Roker Roar Choir practice with the Hylton Castle Barber shop Quartet
   d) Morris Dancing and Cake Decoration in the players lounge.
   e) Wife swapping with Chris Makin
   f) And Rubber Mask pottery and face painting with Eric Gates

"We should look at the local Saturday and Sunday league teams around the area to stop the talent going elsewhere"

? QUIT

50:50

15	$1 MILLION
14	$500,000
13	$250,000
12	$125,000
11	$64,000
10	$32,000
9	$16,000
8	$8,000
7	$4,000
6	$2,000
5	$1,000
4	$500
3	$300
2	$200
1	$100

50:50

What is the best selling drink on Wearside?

A: Craig David

B: News of the World

C: Dusseldorf

D: 9p a bottle, Trampy Blue pop

NUFC MACKEMS·R·SHITE NUFC

THE ROKER CHOKER

It was a night in early September
This was a night we knew we would always remember

Everyone said that we would lose
But Keegan's boys were oh so smooth

We had no official fans on that night
But we were only playing mackem shite

The game was away at Joker Park
Big Ears and Ginger hair in the dark

Ferdie crossed for Beardsley to score
But no one heard the Roker roar

We now started to play with some style
Terry Mac and Kev began to smile

Ferdie scored with all his might
To stick it up the mackem shite

There was now an almighty hush
As the scum left gutted in a rush

Every time Shearer got the ball
The mackem voices began to call

Scum! Scum! they did scream
But Shearer's cock is worth more than their team

The mackems cried but it did no good
It only made the River Wear flood

Cheer up Peter Reid Oh what can it be
To a fat mackem bastard who has just lost his first derby

Peter and Les scored the goals
To put Geordie pride in our souls

Our subs on the bench cost a few bob
Worth more than the scum's first team's squad

What will be said in years to come?
But Howay the Lads they are only mackem Scum

JOKES

What's the definition of mass confusion?
Father's Day in Hendon.

Mick McCarthy is having trouble coaching his players to the standard of the First Division, so he goes to see Harry Redknapp at Portsmouth who'd won promotion the season before on a low budget. The Pompey manager tells Mick that he trains his players mentally as well as physically. He calls Paul Merson over and says, "Paul you are your father's son, but not your brother, who are you?" Paul replies, "It's me." Harry tells Mick to go away and do the same with the sunderland players, so the next day in training he asks Kevin Kilbane the same question. Kevin asks for 24 hours to think about it. Kilbane is worried so he asks Jason McAteer. Jason says, "Well that's simple. It's me." So the next day Kevin Kilbane runs up to McCarthy and says, with a big grin on his face, "It's Jason, It's Jason McAteer." And McCarthy replies, "No it's not it's Paul Merson."

Which sexual position produces the ugliest children?
Ask a Mackem.

Why do the majority of Mackems have moustaches?
So they look like their mothers.

Why did God invent alcohol?
So Mackems could get a shag as well.

How can you tell if a Mackem lass has been using your computer?
There is Tippex on the screen.

What have sunderland football club and Enola Gay both got in common?
They both wasted millions!

What's the difference between a mackem and a Computer?
You only have to punch information into a Computer once.

What's the difference between a Mackem and a Lada?
You can slam the door on a Mackem.

What's the difference between a Mackem and a Hamburger?
There are more balls in a Hamburger.

What's the hardest part of a Cabbage?
A sunderland scarf.

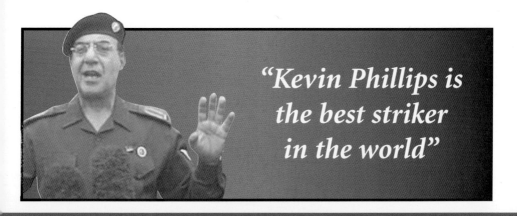

"Kevin Phillips is the best striker in the world"

MY FAMILY PHOTO ALBUM

Hello Marra... This is me like. Douglas Derek Andrews, I'm aged 19 but you can just call me Nigel for short. My Mum reckons I look like Sewpa Kev & Stephen Wright with Glasses. My 17 year old dad reckons I get my looks and brains from him. Sexy girls make me wet my pants. I made a battle ship out of wood last week because I want to be a bus driver when I grow up. I've supported sunderland since I went free with school last year.

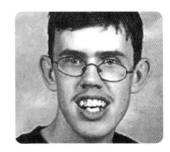

Mum

This is my most recent Mum, four-time divorced Doris. She makes great Cheesy chips. She brings me a different Uncle home every Saturday night. She loves Julio Arca, she's got all of his albums. She went to Netto after watching Kilroy last Friday and we haven't seen her since.

Derek my Step Dad

He used to be a Black Belt in glue sniffing and ran the local Scout group. But now he is under a care order and his application to be a Lollipop man has been rejected. Doesn't really speak to me much, in fact I haven't seen him since my yellow Wellies went missing? Enjoys watching sunderland when his mates from junior school get free tickets.

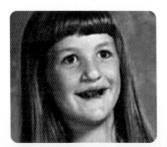

My Stepsister Chantelle

My younger Stepsister Chantelle Bethany Claire Louise has a beautiful smile, ever since she gave her vibrator a blow job. She fancies Sean 'Beckham' Thornton like mad and wants his babies.